GROWING RURAL-URBAN DISPARITY IN UTTARAKHAND

Series Author

S. S. P. Sharma

Nilabja Ghosh
Sabyasachi Kar
Suresh Sharma

NATIONAL INSTITUTE OF RURAL DEVELOPMENT (NIRD)
RAJENDRANAGAR, HYDERABAD

SERIALS PUBLICATIONS
NEW DELHI (INDIA)

First Published - 2008

ISBN: 978-81-8387-202-7

Published by

SERIALS PUBLICATIONS
4830/24, Prahlad Street, Ansari Road
Darya Ganj, New Delhi-110002 (India)
Phone : 23245225
Fax : 91-11-23272135
E-mail: serials@satyam.net.in, w.w.w.serialspublications.com

CONTENTS

PREFACE

The increasing disparity between rural and urban areas in India is a blot on our civilization, particularly in an age when technological advancements and economic developments are improving the average standard of living at a fast pace. With economic reforms ushering in an era of prosperity, studies that focus on the unequal distribution of these gains, which are not reaching the large rural parts of the country, have become essential. The project 'Growing Rural Urban Disparity', that focuses on a number of states in India, is an attempt towards this extremely important aim. This book is based on our research on the new Himalayan state of Uttarakhand, as a part of this broader project. Uttarakhand stands apart from most other states in the project for two reasons. First, the hilly ecology makes the problems, difficulties and prospects of the state significantly different from of the states lying in the plains. Second, being a new state, there is still a void in the availability of information on many issues of significance. These make the work of analyzing the state a challenging one.

We are extremely grateful to NIRD for sponsoring this work and to Shri Chinmay Basu for his guidance. Our thanks go to the Institute of Economic Growth (IEG) and its former director, Professor B.B. Bhattacharya, for the opportunity to do this research and for providing the infrastructural support required. We also thank Professor Kanchan Chopra, the current director of the Institute, for her encouragement and administrative support towards this project. The Coordinator of the project Dr S.S.P. Sharma deserves to be thanked for keeping the communication alive even while conducting his own study. Many individuals contributed to this work. We thank Mr. Sankar Kumar Sankar, Ms. Aneeta Chauhan and their entire team for the field work, Ms. Preeti for preliminary data work and Ms. Kumud Pandey and Mr. Brijendra Singh for their help in the analysis. Mr. S. Sreedharan and Mr. Inder Kumar as usual helped in all computer related issues. Ms Preeti Sahay helped in revising the draft. The usual disclaimer applies.

Nilabja Ghosh
Sabyasachi Kar
Suresh Sharma

FOREWORD

Spatial differences or inequalities in poverty between urban and rural areas are commonly found at the global level. However, determining the disparities between rural and urban areas is more difficult than it might seem, since it is difficult to define what is urban and what is rural. Economists define an area as urban when the economy is characterized by non-extractive occupations, for example, industry, commerce, that benefit particularly from a high population density and the accompanying infrastructure. However, improved transport and the relative reduction in transport costs have made it easier to commute between an urban area and its surrounding rural areas or to migrate temporarily from rural to urban areas.

India has a total population of over 1 billion, of which 28% live in urban areas. There has been growth in the percentage of the urban population residing in large cities: it has increased from 60% in early 1980s to over 65% in the early 1990s. Overall, the growth rate of the urban population has slowed from the record level of 3.8% per annum in the 1970s to 3.1% in the 1980s and 2.7% in the 1990s. The slowing down has been greater in smaller towns. The inequality is increasing both in terms of per capita incomes and other socio-economic indicators. In recent decades, however, both the rates of out-migration from backward states and migration into developed states have been reduced. The decline in out-migration from rural areas in backward states like Bihar, Madhya

Pradesh, Rajasthan and Uttar Pradesh which have high population growth rates presents a serious problem for their absorption in the rural economy. Seasonal and circular migration of labour for employment has become one of the most durable components of the livelihood strategies of people living in rural areas.

During the post 90s, the rural-urban gap is widening. NIRD has taken a longitudinal study in six states in the first phase, i.e. Assam, Bihar, Gujarat, Karnataka, Maharashtra and Uttrakhand. The second phase study in Madhya Pradesh, Orissa, Tamil Nadu and U.P. is going on. From the first phase study, it is reported that the disparity in social consumption in Karnataka and Uttrakhand is less pronounced than in Bihar and Assam. Surprisingly, the disparity in leading states-Gujarat and Maharashtra is increasing. However, the income-increase in rural area is reported almost in all the states but very slow in Bihar. The study was coordinated by S. S. P. Sharma, Professor and Head, Centre for Water and Land Management (CWLM) and completed by the lead institutes of the country–IGIDR, Mumbai (Maharashtra), IRMA, Anand (Gujarat), ISEC, Bangalore (Karnataka) and IGE, Delhi (Uttrakhand). I hope this volume will provide help to the policy makers at the Centre as well as in the states to explore some mechanism to bridge the emerging gap between rural and urban areas in the country.

V. S. Sampath

Hyderabad, **V. S. Sampath**
January, 2008 *Director General*

PART - I

DEVELOPMENT AND DISPARITY IN SOCIAL AND ECONOMIC SECTORS

1

DEVELOPMENT AND DISPARITY

The concept of development is far broader than that of economic growth. The development objectives of a country or a state need to be defined not only in terms of per capita income, but also in terms of adequate access to facilities that confer well-being and capability to the people. These include basic social services like education, health and sanitation and economic and social opportunities for all. Further, without the right institutions and good governance, economic growth does not necessarily translate into welfare for all sections of the people. Clearly, when growth does not lead to less inequality and poverty, it cannot be called development. Thus a fair distribution of the gains acquired through growth is an integral component of development.

In India, the Five-year Plans were aimed at achieving balanced growth and equity right from the beginning of our planned development (Chakravarty, 1987). Although targets and approaches have undergone amendments in this planning process, equity has always remained an important objective. The wave of liberalisation sweeping the world and India in the last few decades shifted the development strategy from the planning process to the powers of the market, which promised higher growth rates and more trickle-down effect to the weaker sections of the economy. Over time however, the limitations of the growth rate as an index of development has been exposed. The multi-dimensional nature of poverty (World Bank, 2001, 2004) and the failures of the market in terms of providing opportunities to the weaker sections of society is now common knowledge. In India, the difference in terms of opportunities between the rural and urban areas is large and growing and this has been a most important factor behind economic disparity in our country. Despite the wide array of poverty eradication and development programmes, the rural sector remains the deprived sector in many ways.

The growing disparity between rural and urban areas that are in geographical proximity with each other, with no significant differences in resource base or natural advantage, can only be an outcome of policy failure. The policy of economic reforms launched in the early 1990s is made up of structural adjustments, privatization, market liberalization and subsequently, also globalization. All these implicitly meant a greater role for the market, a reduction in the size of the government and an intensification of competition-both domestic and international. This set of policies possibly began the reversal of the trends in resource transfer between the rural and urban sectors that was the practice before the reforms. Fiscal flows to the rural sector like subsidies on agricultural inputs were brought down. Water and electricity that had earlier been free utilities for farmers began to be priced ostensibly to encourage efficiency in agriculture. Banks moved towards prudential norms and curbed their risky and less lucrative lending. The volume of credit to agriculture and small enterprises that had earlier constituted 'priority sector lending' in the Indian economy was adversely affected by the process. This is not to say that the reforms did not hold any promise for the rural sector. The structural adjustment packages proposed to set the prices 'right' in favour of agriculture, the main occupation of rural people, that seemed to have suffered 'implicit' taxation in the earlier regulated regime (Gulati and Kelly, 1999). Agricultural trade liberalization held a promise for export markets that would benefit farmers. These arguments have however been countered with others (see Vakulabharanam, 2005) that did not foresee any significant gains for the farmers from these reforms.

Partly as a result of this scepticism, the post-reform period saw a renewed emphasis on poverty eradication programmes and in particular, wage employment programmes. Further, the change of the price-subsidy regime was in turn supplanted by several institutional reorganisations. In this context, the most important change was that in rural governance embodied in the three-tier Panchayati Raj system that received constitutional sanction in 1993. Of course, the effects of decentralisation of governance through elected panchayats on rural welfare and equity have not been an unqualified success and this debate is as yet unresolved (Johnson, 2005). Moreover, little note is taken of the gains in rural areas as a part of the nation's growth, prosperity and technological development. Academic discourses and sometimes, electoral failures have drawn attention towards the distress of poorer farmers, the indifferent attitude of the new financial institutions in terms of their lending to agricultural sector, the poor growth of agricultural output and the deceleration of rural employment. On the positive side, some villages have grown into urban centres but even the pace of urbanisation itself has slowed in the reform period. Migration from rural to urban sectors and remittance in the other direction continue to be the main means of sectoral diffusion.

THEORIES OF GROWTH, DEVELOPMENT, INEQUALITY AND POVERTY

The issue of rural urban disparity can be viewed in the general context of economic inequalities and there is a rich and voluminous literature on this issue. The impact of the growth process on the rate of inequality has been the subject of a long debate. The empirically observed inverted U type relationship between economic growth and inequality (Kuzent (1955)) provides a rationale for tolerating some increases in inequality at the initial stages of growth. In the literature on development economics, Ragnar Nurkse (1953) vicious circle of poverty and Gunnar Myrdal (1957) cumulative causation are stronger theories of inequality that propose that growing inequality will be sustained in the development process by keeping the poorer regions or individuals in a state of stagnation while the developed counterparts prosper and grow. Lipton's (1977) thesis of a pro-urban bias being embedded in most development programmes, focuses specifically on rising rural-urban inequality. On the other hand, the neoclassical growth theory predicts the convergence of regional incomes implying that growth-oriented policies might in fact be a way to end inequality. Further optimism comes from theories of economic geography (Elizondo and Krugman, 1992) that postulate that economic activities will spatially redistribute themselves more evenly within the nations as the economy opens up. There are empirical evidences of the claim that growth benefits both the rich and the poor (Dollar and Kray, 2001, Sale-i-Martin, 2002). However, empirical studies also note increasing inequality across countries and across households within countries. Conversely, inequality is found to adversely affect growth itself through political instability, credit cycles, investment weariness and limited development capabilities, making equity itself an important precondition for growth.

After more than a decade of reforms in India, we are currently experiencing growth rates around eight per cent, much higher than those ever achieved earlier. At the same time, the reforms have opened up debates on the issue of inequality. Apprehensions have arisen about the distribution of the gains and the trends in inequality in the country. The declining role of the centralized planning process, the structural changes since the reforms and specifically the deceleration of public investment arising out of fiscal constraints have given rise to widespread concern about the resultant increases in regional inequality. The Indian growth performance has already been shown to be significantly uneven across the states (Bhattacharya and Saktivel, 2003). The economy has shown divergence across states not only at the aggregate level but also at the level of activity i.e., agriculture, industry and services (Kar and Sakthivel, 2003). Several studies applied and tested the neo-classical thesis of growth convergence among Indian states to find out if poorer regions (states) were catching up with the rich ones. The evidences were more in favour of (conditional) divergence of the states (Marjit and Mitra, 1996, Rao, Shand and Kalirajan, 1999).

The development experiences of various Asian countries have demonstrated that poverty is an outcome of not only economic processes but also of political and social phenomena (Deolalikar et al 2002). Conventionally, poverty is measured by income or expenditure with respect to a specified level called the poverty line that represents a subsistence level of income or consumption. Moving beyond income poverty, Sen visualised (Sen, 1999, 2003) a wider dimension where the poor are deprived of the basic right and opportunity to do basic things in life and suffer a 'social unfreedom' that disables them from participating democratically in society. His theories focus on human development that involves acquisition of important capabilities with no discrimination based on caste, region or sex. In particular, women have been historically marginalized in society and hence gender becomes an important dimension in development. Several backward classes have suffered the effects of historical discrimination. Due to its impersonal nature, the market continues to overlook the interests of these classes. Moving away from consumer based notions of welfare, there are more sophisticated concepts of well-being now emerging in the literature that are much more humane and composite and considers both man and environment (Dasgupta, 2001). Freedom from poverty and insecurity and ability to participate in society are usually considered to be part of human well-being. In the global policy sphere, the leading international development institutions, together with all the countries of the world, have set for themselves eight goals of equitable development known as the Millennium Development Goals (MDGs) with a target date of 2015. While the situation in less developed areas - including most of rural India - often fall far short of satisfactory levels of development, it is now understood that the process of development could be time consuming. However, the need of the hour is determined and planned action and this is clear from the following quote from the United Nations website, "...We will have time to reach the Millennium Development Goals-worldwide and in most, or even all, individual countries –but only if we break with business as usual. We cannot win overnight. Success will require sustained action across the entire decade between now and the deadline. It takes time to train the teacher, nurses and engineers; to build the roads, schools and hospitals; to grow the small and large businesses able to create the jobs and income needed. So we must start now. And we must more than double global development assistance over the next few years. Nothing less will help to achieve the Goals..."

Rural Urban Linkages

The whole issue of comparing the rural and urban sectors is not meant to infer that the relation between the sectors is simply one of competition. While a competitive element is implied in allocating scarce public resources among sectors involving bargaining among different groups of people and political entities, the relationship that binds the two sectors is largely one of complementarity. The linkages between the sectors and that between agriculture and industry are conceptualized in theory as those based on close interdependencies. The rural sector is expected to supply food and raw materials for urban life and activities and also surplus labour power (as in the celebrated Lewis Model) and in turn demand consumer and industry-produced goods from the other. Prosperity in one sector benefits the other, as each constitutes a market for the other's product. In reality, the relationship of inter-dependences often exhibits a degree of asymmetry. The urban center close to a group of villages generally acts as a hub for most purposes through which products, humans, skills and knowledge flow in and out. They form an intermediary between the villages and the outer world. However, modern information technology enables a certain amount of bypassing or 'leap-fogging', especially relevant to less accessible areas. Indians live in more than 5 lakh villages of small habitations and often they are scattered spatially. It is desirable for these villages to be self-sufficient in basic amenities for a quality day-to-day life. However, in many areas it becomes uneconomic to provide each village with all necessary amenities of a good life due to the diseconomies of scale. For example, basic schooling and primary health facility could be made available within reach of rural areas but provision of expert knowledge and specialized consultation in many villages may not be scale-effective. Similarly a center of convergence is required for rural output to be distributed nationally and urban centers play this role. Materials, expertise, technology and equipment necessary for education, health care, civic amenities, modern life are brought from elsewhere in India or from other countries through the agency of government or market and urban centers often serve as a reserve, so that the surrounding rural areas can acquire or access them cheaply, quickly and timely. Similarly primary products generated in villages find a market not only in the urban centre but could reach other more distant markets through agencies operating from urban centers that have the capability to procure, stock and market them. Naturally, more of non-primary sector employments are generated in urban centers because of multiple activities and rural people also find employment opportunities in cities and towns. The urban centers thrive not only from the rural market, rural sourcing and rural surplus manpower and knowledge but also enjoy the external effects of the environmental, social and economic conditions prevailing in neighboring areas.

A crucial linkage between the urban centers and neighboring villages is provided by communication through good roads or railways whereby villagers are expected to commute to the urban areas for higher education, medical advice, selling farm produce, purchase of household goods or simply for a living. The rural urban interaction also helps exchange of ideas and demonstrations affecting rural ways of life. It is important that the urban centres should be within easy reach and be well connected with the villages. They should serve well as vibrant and effective centres for the hinterland. In this model it is the failure of policy if the urban centre stagnates or thrives for its own sake or if the synergic relations flourish in a narrow radius. Worse still is the case where political or economic mechanisms meant to strengthen the rural-urban linkages actually encourage disparity between the two sectors.

The structure of the economy is undergoing changes with newer sectors coming up. Agriculture is losing importance as a dominant source of income, though a large section of people are still locked in cultivation or farm labour. The poor income potentials of agriculture as a profession and the demonstration of effect of urban life are luring many members of farmer families to look for other pastures. The National Sample Survey Organization (NSSO) survey in India reported that about 40% of the farmers would like to move from agriculture due to various reasons. Other constraints on living also make a rural life unattractive. These are caused by shortfalls in public policy as also market failure. The dispersion of habitations, poor communication and low purchasing power are some of the factors that inhibit operations of the private sector in the rural economy. Table 1 shows that the rural sector in India fell behind the urban sector in several social and economic indicators. Further, some additional issues have gained attention that relate to both the rural and urban sectors and have critical implications for development. Some of these issues are (i) Transition in population growth and approach of replacement rate (ii) Adverse sex ratios (iii) Problems of employment and diversification (iv)

Table 1
Rural Urban Disparity of Development in India

Development indicators	*Rural*	*Urban*
Crude birth rate	25.6	19.1
Crude death rate	8.1	6.0
Total fertility rate	3.2	2.1
Infant mortality rate	64	40
Literacy rate(above 7years) 200	55.6	79.5
Attendance (net) rate in Elementary (grade1-V111) school	60.6	71.1
Households with toilet (%)	61.6	73.8
Monthly per capita consumption Expenditures (Rs.)	558.8	1052.4

Source: (i) Family Welfare Statistics in India, 2006.
(ii) Multiple Indicator Survey, 2000.

Greater importance to social sector issues like education, health and civic amenities of life (v) Issues of gender equality and women. This study on Uttarakhand focuses on disparities in general and rural-urban disparities in particular and keeps in view the issues of national importance mentioned above.

UTTARAKHAND: AN OVERVIEW

Formed in November 9, 2000, Uttarakhand is India's 27th state and one of the most recently formed ones. It is carved out of the hilly region of the largest and most populous state in India namely, Uttar Pradesh. Located at the foothills of the Himalayas, it shares borders with China and Nepal and is a neighbour to Himachal Pradesh, Uttar Pradesh, Punjab, and Haryana. It is sprawled over 53.5 thousand sq. kms. with less than 2 % of India's geographical area (Graph 1). The region is home to rich bio-diversity and to the early courses of most of the rivers that drain and enrich northern India. The new state, a culmination of a long-standing struggle for separate statehood, represents the aspirations of its people to usher in all round socio-economic development. The capital of the state is Dehradun. The population is mostly Hindu

Graph 1
Geographical and Population Comparison

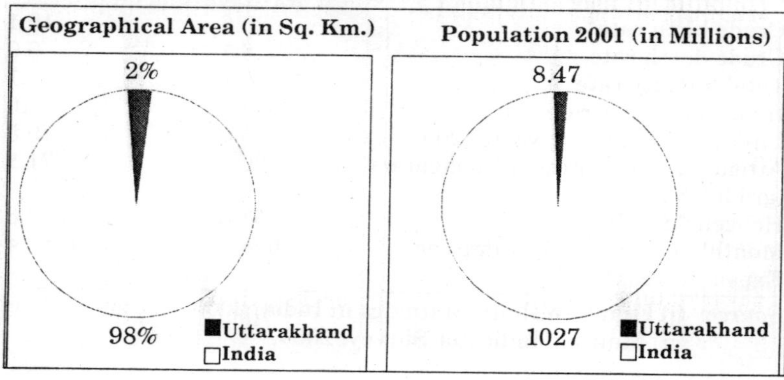

with a small percentage of Muslims and Sikhs. The share of scheduled tribe (ST) population is only 3%, (Table 2) which is less than other hilly states especially those of the north-east, while its scheduled caste (SC) population is second only to Himachal within the hilly states.

Table 2
Social Composition of the Population

Muslim	11.9
Christian	3.2
Sikh	2.5
SC	17.9
ST	3.0

Source: Census of India, 1991.

Uttarakhand is a hilly state located on the Himalayas in the northern parts (latitudes 28^0 North to 310 North) in India. The elevation extends from approximately 300 to 7000 meters above sea level. The highest peak here is Nanda Devi (7817 m) in the Chamoli District and Kedarnath and Trishul are other peaks. Glaciers include Gangotri, Pindari and Khatling several important rivers like Ganga, Yamuna and Ramganga have their upper courses in this state. Starting from the foothills in the South it extends to snow clad mountains in the north. The entire state forms part of the Central Himalayas. The state is interspersed with rivers, deep valleys, glaciers, flower valleys and high peaks the state presents a very pristine, pure and picturesque environment supplemented by the dense Himalayan forests that cover the lower slopes.

A majority of the thirteen districts in Uttarakhand are hilly. Haridwar, Dehradun, Nainital and Udham Singh Nagar are the only districts that have significant parts in the plains. Pauri, the Headquarter of Pauri-Garhwal district is situated at a height of 1814 metres and Tehri, the headquarter of Tehri-Garhwal district is at an altitude of 770 mts It is situated at the confluence of Bhagirathi and Bhilangana rivers or a hilly valley in the foothills. Haridwar is situated on the banks of river Ganga and at the foothills of Shivalik Mountains. Almora is a hill district in the central Kumaon region of Uttarakhand. Numerous rivers like Ganga Jamuna, Bhagirathi, and Mandakini water the area and provide scenic confluences. Kedarnath, Badrinath and glaciers like Gangotri and Jamunotri are tourist spots. Of the thirteen districts, four are new and carved out of other districts listed in Census 1991 as shown in Table 3.

Table 3
New Districts 2001 Census

New Districts 2001	Rudraprayag	Champawat	Bageshwar	Udham Singh Nagar
Parent Districts 1991	Chamoli Tehri Garhwal Garhwal	Pithoragarh	Almora	Nainital

The state has two administrative divisions, Garhwal and Kumaon. The districts Almora, Pithoragarh, Nainital and the newly constituted Bageshwar, Champawat, Udham Singh Nagar form the Kumaon division while Uttrakashi, Chamoli, Dehradun, Pauri Garhwal, Tehri Garhwal and newly formed Rudraprayag and Haridwar districts fall under the Garhwal Division.

The state is further divided into 46 tehsils, and 95 blocks as of 2001. There are only 4 cities with a population of 1 lakh or more and they are mostly in the foot hills or plains–Haridwar UA, Dehradun UA, Haldwani–Kathgodam UA and Roorkee UA. Besides these, there are 73 towns with less than 1 lakh population that include well-known spots like Rishikesh UA in Dehradun, Ranikhat CB in Almora, Joshimath HB in Chamoli and Gangotri NP in Uttarkhashi. In the wake of the construction of the Tehri Dam, a new township of New Tehri was developed at a height of 1500 meters above sea level. As per Revenue Department's records, the revenue villages number up to 16583 in the state. It has 15669 habitat villages, 6561-Gram Sabhas, and 673 Nyay Panchayats (Table 4).

Table 4
Administrative Units in Uttarakhand 2001, 2005

Administrative Units	*Unit*	*Details*
Districts	Number	13
Tehsil	Number	49
Towns	Number	73
Gram Sabha	Number	6561
Nyay Panchayat	Number	673
Blocks	Number	95
Habitat Village	Number	15669
Revenue Village	Number	16583
Cities (1 lakh + Population)	Unit	4
Gram Panchayats	Unit	6950
Muncipal Boards	Unit	32

Source: 2001 Uttarakhand Rajya-Vividh Soochnay, JRC 2005.

Uttarakhand has little variety in the social composition of its population. Hindus make up nearly 90% of the populations and only Haridwar, Nainital and Dehradun have less than 96% of Hindus. Muslims-making up 12% of the population–are found mostly in Haridwar. The proportions of Muslims are highest in Haridwar and Nainital (45%). It exceeds 10% in rural Haridwar and Dehradun and urban Haridwar, Nainital and Garhwal. Rural Nainital also has some Sikh population but the Christian population is very small and constitutes less than 1% in most cases. In most districts the Scheduled Caste (SC) population varies from 13% to 17% with more than 20% share in found in Uttarkashi, Pithoragarh, Almora and Haridwar. Unlike other hilly states, the share of Scheduled Tribes is small but together with the Scheduled Castes, the backward sections constitute more than 20% in Nainital, Chamoli and Dehradun (Table 5) apart from the above four districts.

Table 5
Composition of Population by Religion (%) and by Scheduled Castes and Scheduled Tribes, 1991

District	*Area*	*Hindu*	*Muslim*	*Religion Christian*	*Sikh*	*Others*	*Castes / Tribes*	
							Scheduled Castes	*Scheduled Tribes*
Uttarkashi	Rural	98.49	0.67	0.03	0.08	0.73	23.54	1.01
	Urban	95.31	3.87	0.19	0.41	0.22	12.97	0.35
	Total	98.26	0.90	0.04	0.10	0.69	22.78	0.96
Chamoli	Rural	99.16	0.50	0.02	0.20	0.12	17.58	1.92
	Urban	96.49	2.96	0.08	0.14	0.32	16.61	5.76
	Total	98.92	0.72	0.03	0.19	0.14	17.49	2.26
Tehri Garhwal	Rural	99.31	0.62	0.03	0.02	0.03	14.44	0.10
	Urban	93.83	4.35	0.36	1.00	0.45	10.25	0.20
	Total	99.00	0.83	0.05	0.07	0.05	14.20	0.11
Dehradun	Rural	84.90	12.58	0.44	1.39	0.69	15.15	15.88
	Urban	85.67	6.71	1.30	4.52	1.80	11.67	0.60
	Total	85.29	9.63	0.87	2.97	1.25	13.40	8.20
Garhwal	Rural	98.76	0.93	0.13	0.13	0.06	13.91	0.23
	Urban	85.75	12.18	1.09	0.47	0.51	10.62	0.18
	Total	97.21	2.27	0.24	0.17	0.11	13.52	0.22

Contd..

District	*Area*	*Religion*					*Castes/Tribes*	
		Hindu	*Muslim*	*Christian*	*Sikh*	*Others*	*Scheduled Castes*	*Scheduled Tribes*
Pithorgarh	Rural	99.63	0.17	0.11	0.02	0.07	20.83	2.89
	Urban	93.66	4.57	1.23	0.46	0.07	15.67	7.53
	Total	99.19	0.50	0.19	0.06	0.07	20.45	3.23
Almora	Rural	99.62	0.24	0.06	0.03	0.05	22.44	0.26
	Urban	90.13	6.36	2.15	1.04	0.13	15.95	1.30
	Total	99.02	0.63	0.19	0.09	0.06	22.02	0.33
Nainital	Rural	79.34	9.15	0.34	11.03	0.14	18.02	8.49
	Urban	68.51	27.75	0.45	3.06	0.23	11.22	0.39
	Total	75.80	15.23	0.37	8.43	0.17	15.80	5.84
Haridwar	Rural	65.53	33.52	0.04	0.85	0.06	26.46	0.26
	Urban	74.67	22.37	0.48	1.79	0.68	10.71	0.01
	Total	68.36	30.07	0.18	1.14	0.25	21.58	0.18

Source: Population Foundation of India, New Delhi.

Prospects and Problems of a Hilly State

Uttarakhand is situated mostly in the mountains with a little more than 7% of the state in the plains. It is a state that combines various strengths and weaknesses owing primarily to its geography. Only 11.5% of the area is available for cultivation and 63% is under forest cover. Irrigation potential is extremely limited. Land degradation is a serious problem as the slopes make the region vulnerable to soil and water erosion and also to landslides. Earthquake is another natural calamity that hits parts of the state.

Like any hilly region with its heights and slopes, this state is constrained by its own geography that hinders development of industry on a large scale, limits the use of modern mechanized and input intensive agriculture and necessitates conservation of forest resources both for the stability of its own ecology and the deep interaction it has with the adjoining plains. The state has to share the interests of the people of India at large and provide an ecological service to the country by conserving the Himalayas. The forests covering over 60% area contribute to India's forest coverage of 22%.

The topology has a profound impact on the economy's structure. The state is predominantly rural. About 74% of the population lives in the rural areas (Census 2001) and about 90% of the state's population depends on agriculture. Urbanization is largely confined to plain regions. Agriculture contributes about two third of the net domestic product of the state. Most of the industries are small-scale or forest based and there are only a few heavy industries. There is a high degree of spatial imbalance with more than 62% of state Net Domestic Product coming from three major towns Dehradun, Haridwar and Nainital. Agriculture mostly involves food grains with little value addition. The mountain topology makes transportation difficult and costly and the resultant urgency for self-sufficiency has partly contributed to subsistence agriculture. Private investment is poor. The population density is low with the three districts of Uttarkashi, Chamoli and Pithoragarh having some of the lowest population densities in the country. The sparse and scattered population creates difficulty for a market to function. Social development has also been slowed down by this inaccessibility coupled with the limitation of the state's finances. About 84% of the village settlements (nearly 90% in Paori Garhwal, Pithoragarh, Chamoli, Tehri Garhwal and Almora) have population sizes of less than 500 and hardly 0.5% of the villages in most districts have more than 2000 population (Table 6). The scattered small size settlements in hill regions offer a formidable challenge to development programmes and market formation.

Table 6
Percentage Distribution of Villages by Population Size

District	*<200*	*0-500*	*500-999*	*1000-1998*	*2000-4999*	*5000+*
Uttarkashi	39.1	81.9	14.7	3.1	0.3	-
Chamoli	53.0	87.7	9.8	2.4	0.1	-
Tehri	47.3	85.7	12.4	1.8	-	0.1
Dehradun	36.9	71.4	12.7	9.4	4.6	2.0
Pauri	68.2	94.1	4.1	0.6	0.2	-
Pithoragarh	61.0	89.7	7.8	2.1	0.4	-
Almora	52.3	87.9	9.8	2.0	0.2	-
Nainital	35.0	65.2	18.3	11.9	4.1	0.5
Haridwar	9.7	24.8	22.5	26.2	23.3	3.2
Uttarakhand	51.6	83.7	10.4	4.1	1.6	0.2

Source: Census 1991.

The high altitude, wild life endowments, fragile ecology and seismic possibilities in the state make most development projects risky. Most notably, the Tehri Dam promising considerable electricity generation and irrigation potential was the centre of an important environmental agitation that delayed its construction. Uttarakhand also carries the legacies of the administration of Uttar Pradesh, which embody a vast mass of contradictions and diversities, social, political and economic in nature. The economic and social conditions also symbolise to a large extent the relative indifference that rural India received in the years of development.

The state also has a number of comparative advantages. It has rich mineral deposits. Tourism is a dominant activity based on the scenic beauty and the mountainous topography. The religious attraction of the numerous places of worship even in remote regions has drawn tourists and travellers now and through ages. The place is considered by many to be the abode of Gods and Goddesses. The Himalayan forest with their wild life and National Parks impart additional attraction. Human resource is the most valuable asset. The state is remarkable for its hard working, progressive and independent minded (Joshi, 1995) people, their activism demonstrated through the famous Chipko movement on commercial forestry, the environmental movements like that surrounding the Tehri dam and the struggle for the identity of new state and districts. The state produced competent and intellectual manpower for the country although many have migrated to the plains for their vocation. The state surpasses many other states in possessing a literate and educated population.

The forests with their bio-diversity can be a rich source of useful products like medicinal plants and the hill climate provide for tropical, exotic, off-season and temperate crops in demand elsewhere and which have crucial linkage with the food processing industry. Dehradun, Haridwar and adjoining areas are known for their good quality rice. Light non-polluting industries are an option. The state has considerable potential for hydro-power due to the numerous streams and rivers and the

Tehri Dam. The failure of the green revolution that brought high productivity in the plains now appears to be an opportunity for organic farming. Proximity to metros like Delhi is an added market advantage. Employment prospects have been low in the hilly state leading to migration to plains and development of the state on its own strengths deserves priority. Harnessing the advantages and build up of communication both through efficient transportation and modern electronic and satellite based technologies are viewed to be the way to development.

Rural and Urban Sectors in Uttarakhand

There is no uniform definition of rural and urban areas in the world. The definition used in this study is the same as Census 2001. A place is designated as 'urban' if the following criteria are satisfied.

(a) All places with a (i) Municipal Corporation (ii) Municipality (iii) Cantonment Board (iv) Notified Town Area Committee etc.

(b) All other places having (i) A minimum population of 5000 (ii) At least 75% of the male working population engaged in non-agricultural pursuits and (iii) A density of population of at least 400 per sq. km.

Table 7

Rural Population in Uttarakhand and India (Millions)

Region	*Population 1991*	*Population 2001*	*Rural% 1991*	*Rural% 2001*
Uttarakhand	7.11	8.48	76	74.41
India	856	1019	74.3	72.2

Source: Rural Development Statistics, NIRD and Census 2001.

Uttarakhand comprises of less than 1% of India's population. The population of Uttarakhand increased by 1.4 millions i.e., by 19% between 1991 and 2001 (Table 7).

The share of rural population came down from 76% to 74%. Due to population increase certain villages were re-designated as towns. Haridwar is the most populated district followed by Dehradun, Udhan Singh Nagar and Nainital though Uttakashi, Chamoli and Pithoragarh are large districts in area (Table 8). The four districts namely Haridwar, Dehradun, Udham Singh Nagar and Nainital gained in terms of the share in population over 1991 (Table 9). The hilly districts lost in terms of the share of population from 47.8% to 44.3% while the districts with large parts in the plains gained from 52% to 56%. In the hills, only Uttarkashi also made a small gain of 0.1%. Haridwar has the largest rural population and Dehradun also comes within the first four districts in terms of rural population.

Table 8
Area and Population of Districts, 2001

District	*Head-quarters*	*Total Population*	*Rural Population*	*Urban Population*	*Area Sq.Km.*
Haridwar	Haridwar	1444213	998550	445663	2360
Dehradun	Dehradun	1279083	601965	677118	3088
Udham Singh Nagar	Rudrapur	1234548	831407	403141	2908
Nainital	Nainital	762912	493126	269786	3860
Garhwal	Pauri	696851	606629	90222	5399
Almora	Almora	630446	576497	53949	3082
Tehri Garhwal	Tehri Garhwal	604608	546133	58475	4080
Pithorgarh	Pithoragarh	462149	406025	56124	7100
Chamoli	Chamoli	369198	319613	49585	7614
Uttarkashi	Uttarkashi	294179	271255	22924	8016
Bageshwar	Bageshwar	249453	241650	7803	2303
Rudraprayag	Rudraprayag	227461	224740	2721	1891
Champawat	Champawat	224461	191727	32734	1781
Uttarakhand	Dehradun	8479562	6309317	2170245	53331

Source: Census 2001.
Note: Districts are ranked by the population sizes.

Table 9 gives area and population shares of districts ranked by total population. Haridwar, Udham Singh Nagar and Dehradun are three of the more urbanised districts in terms of population, but lead in rural absolute population as well. Similarly, some of the districts which have high shares of population in the rural sector such as Rudraprayag, Bageshwar and Uttarkashi have relatively small sized rural populations as well as a low share of the state population. Dehradun, Haridwar and US Nagar have higher shares of state population in the rural sector but have some of the highest levels of urbanisation. Thus, more populated districts are more urbanized.

More than 36% of the families in the state are registered as below poverty line (Garibi Rekha or BPL) as notified by state and local governments. Most districts have high share of families in this category and Uttarkashi has the highest record. In general the hilly districts also including Chamoli, Tehri Garhwal have Bageshwar have some of the highest shares of registration of BPL families. These are also districts with high shares of rural population.

Table 9 also demarcates the districts by their geography. As noted, the four districts made up of substantial plain regions are more urbanized and the share of rural population in the group is a mere 62% compared to 90% in the hill districts. Although these districts constitute less than 30% of the state's area, they contain 55% of the state's population. On the other hand the hill districts make up 77% of the area and 54% of the rural population. The rural urban demarcation is therefore also manifested in the geographical demarcation. In many parts of this study, the disparity between rural and urban areas is manifested in terms of the difference between the hilly districts and the districts lying substantially in the plains.

Table 9
Population and Area Shares in Hill and Plain Districts (%)

District	*District share in state Population*				*Geo-graphic area*	*Rural-BPL families share in district*	*Rural share of district popula-tion*
	Total		*Rural*	*Urban*			
	1991	*2001*	*2001*	*2001*		*2001*	*2001*
Haridwar	16.07	17.03	15.83	20.54	4.43	17.58	69.14
Dehradun	14.42	15.08	9.54	31.20	5.79	34.22	47.06
Udham Singh Nagar	13.58	14.56	13.18	18.58	5.45	36.68	67.35
Nainital	8.07	9.00	7.82	12.43	7.24	30.55	64.64
Substantially Plain Districts	*52.14*	*55.67*	*46.36*	*82.74*	*22.91*	*28.62*	*61.96*
Garhwal	9.43	8.22	9.61	4.16	10.12	26.74	87.05
Almora	8.59	7.43	9.14	2.49	5.78	36.58	91.44
Tehri Garhwal	7.32	7.13	8.66	2.69	7.65	56.53	90.33
Pithorgarh	5.86	5.45	6.44	2.59	13.31	30.81	87.86
Chamoli	4.57	4.35	5.07	2.28	14.28	51.69	86.57
Uttarkashi	3.37	3.47	4.30	1.06	15.03	68.51	92.21
Bageshwar	3.21	2.94	3.83	0.36	4.32	41.63	96.87
Rudraprayag	2.82	2.68	3.56	0.13	3.55	37.37	98.80
Champawat	2.68	2.65	3.04	1.51	3.34	37.35	85.42
Hilly Districts	*47.85*	*44.33*	*53.64*	*17.26*	*77.38*	*41.79*	*90.04*
Uttarakhand	100	100	100	100	100	36.44	74.41

STRUCTURE OF THE BOOK

This book attempts to study the rural-urban disparity that exists in the Himalayan State of Uttarakhand. The book has two parts. The first part, consisting of chapters one, two and three, analyses the nature of development and disparity in the state and is based on secondary data sources. It aims to study the (i) status of the state and the districts in a comparative light, (ii) direction of movement in the last one decade (iii) situation and programmes related to the rural sector wherever the availability of data makes it possible. The sources of data availed for this section are (i) state level or district level aggregate data on Uttarakhand where the State Planning Board made it accessible (ii) Census data at the district level where available (in all cases rural urban demarcation of information not available) (iii) National Family Health Survey (NFHS) data wherever reported (iv) private sources like information compiled by Jagran Research Centre and (v) Seventh all India education survey of NCERT. Chapter two, which focuses on economic development looks at the general development status, the structural make up of the economy and the occupational patterns. Physical infrastructure formation is also examined. Comparison of standards of living across different social and income groups is attempted. The chapter also discusses the main activity of the rural sector namely agriculture, the possibilities emerging and the state of rural development programmes. The progress of agriculture and effective rural development will help in reducing economic disparity. Chapter three, which focuses on social sectors looks at demographic indicators and social development. Various vital rate indicators such as population growth rate, sex ratio, population density, birth rate and death rate and infant mortality rate are examined. Social development in the area of education, health and quality of life is examined at possible disaggregate levels.

The second part consisting of chapters four, five and six focuses on rural-urban disparity in Uttarakhand. It is based on data from secondary sources (chapter four) and also from a primary survey carried out in the state (chapters five and six). Chapter four analyses both social and economic disparity. The analysis of social disparity is based on various secondary data sources. The analysis of economic disparity uses the monthly per capita consumption expenditure as a proxy for income and calculates measure of inequality between the two sectors. This measure is calculated for two periods to gauge the movement of rural urban inequality in consumption over time. Chapter five describes the methodology of the primary survey, which is conducted in three purposively selected districts. For each case an urban centre is drawn and rural areas in its periphery at varying distances to the centre are selected. Households are selected from the urban centre and from each of the villages comprising the rural area by stratified random sampling. The information is summarised for the rural and urban sectors and for the individual districts. Based on this cross-section of data rural-urban disparity is studied in chapter six. This chapter analyses in details the disparity in education, health and quality of life in the state. Chapter seven draws conclusions from the study.

2

ECONOMIC DEVELOPMENT

In this chapter we present a general background of the state's economy, exploring its problems, advantages and challenges: Further, where possible, the exposition touches on implications on the urbanized districts in the plains and the hill districts and on the rural and urban sectors.

THE HIMALAYAN ENVIRONMENT AND ECOLOGY

Economic development is crucially dependent on the resource endowments and the technological possibilities in an area. Uttarakhand is extremely well endowed in natural resources including forests, minerals, water and human resources but the topography of the state imposes huge barriers to conventional technologies and textbook approaches to development. Lying on the laps of the Himalayas, the slopes have impeded large-scale industrialization and the entry of the green revolution. They have provided a formidable challenge to most government programmes and hindered formation of markets. Any development project has to wade its way through a web of conflicting impact on humans and ecology, on short-term gains and long-term sustainability of development. The ecology is highly fragile manifested by the high erosion of soil, run-offs, landslides, mudslides etc. The ecological obligations of the state include the preservation of the watersheds and upper courses of major rivers that enrich the plains, the preservation of forest coverage and wild life to the country at large and maintain the natural beauty, veneration and excitement that the state holds for many. Uttarakhand thus feels the compulsion to choose projects and technology with great caution, not only for its own benefit but also for the country at large.

As a result of the difficult terrain, the extent of industrialization has been poor and agriculture remains the mainstay of the people. Industry and infrastructure development had to seek a balance with the protection of wild life. Even in the agricultural sector, there are conflicts between output expansion and environmental considerations. More intensive cultivation, grazing and forestry cause siltation, floods, landslides, and pollution downstream. Forestry, which was once an important activity, has now come under tighter regulatory controls. Sustainability is not just a 'buzz word' for the state's development but a way of life.

As a result of the lack of overall development, Uttarakhand has become a migration prone state where economic compulsions draw male members to the plains and sometimes to neighboring states, leading to a unique sociology and a dualism between the hills and the plains. This dualism is manifest in the concentration of activities in the limited plain regions of the state. It has generated a sharp contrast in the development between the hill and the plain areas and in their levels of urbanization. Moreover, the migration has its gender implications reflected in the high sex ratio in the hilly districts and women's role and responsibilities in these areas. Development in the hills therefore has special implications for women.

SOURCES OF INCOME AND DISPARITY

Uttarakhand carries the legacy of the larger state Uttar Pradesh and the achievement of statehood initiated a new period of development of its economy. The Net domestic product (NDP) at current prices was recorded at Rs 11,000 crores in 1997-98 posting a 17% increase over 1993-94 while the per capita NDP also rose by 9%. (Table 1). Income generation is dominated by the agricultural sector but even here the rural districts are totally out-shadowed by the urban ones. Agriculture is mostly subsistence farming and only two districts that have large segments of land in the plains and are much more urbanised-Nainital and Dehradun-generate surpluses. Around two-third of the state's output measured by the Net Domestic Product (NDP) comes from agriculture while about 20% comes from the manufacturing sector, which is again mostly from Nainital and Dehradun districts. The contribution to output is less than 5% from hilly districts like Chamoli and Uttarkashi. Forestry contributes 9% of NDP although forest coverage is very high (Graph 1).

Table 1

Increase in Net Domestic Product in Uttarakhand over Time

Year	*NDP Current price Rs. crores*	*NDP Change % at 1993-94 price*	*Per capita NDP Current price Rs.*	*Per capita NDP Change % at 1993-94 price*
1993-94	6652		9053	
1997-98	11342	17.2	13989	8.9

Source: Computed from state Government data (*www.gov.ua.nic.in*).

There is significant regional concentration of income generated in all the three sectors. The three districts Nainital, Haridwar and Udham Singh Nagar contribute as much as 58% of the primary sector's contribution to the NDP. Thus the hilly districts, despite their rural character, do not make significant contributions even in the agricultural sector (Graph 1(b)). Similarly, Dehradun, Udham Singh Nagar and Haridwar contribute 64% of the secondary sector's contribution and Dehradun, Nainital,

Haridwar and Udham Singh Nagar contribute 62% of the tertiary sector's contribution to the NDP (Graph 1a).

Graph 1(a)
Sector Distribution in NDDP
(Rs. Cr.) at 1993-94 Constant Prices in 1997-98

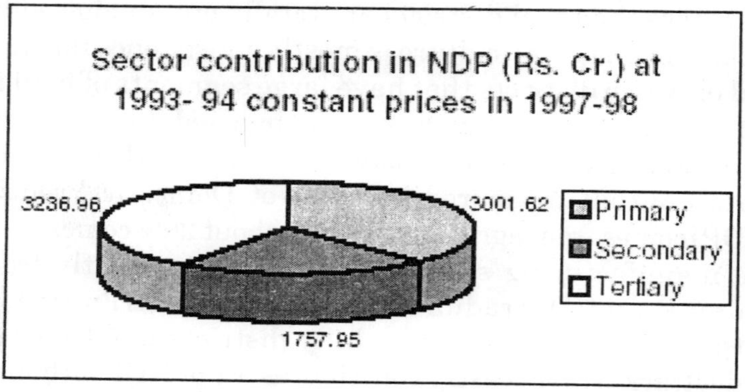

Source: State Planning Department, Government of Uttarakhand.

Graph 1(b)
Share of Commodity Sector (Activities)

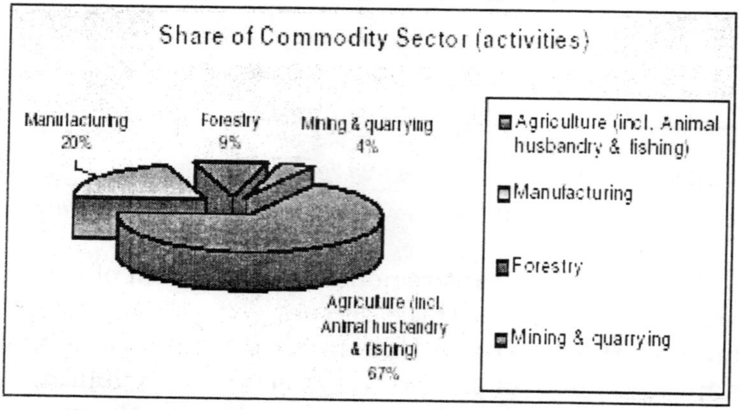

Source: Development of Uttarakhand G.S.Metha.

Inter-district variations (Graph 2(a) and (b)) in net district domestic product (NDDP) are large. Nainital, Dehradun, U.S. Nagar and Haridwar lead in total NDDP

Nainital has the highest per capita NDDP (Rs. 20610) followed by Uttarkashi (Rs. 16497), and Haridwar (Rs. 16803) whereas Chamoli (Rs. 10512) and Almora (Rs. 10367) have much lower per capita NDDP. In Uttarkashithe population size affects the per capita income. Dehradun and Haridwar account for 57% of the state's growth in NDDP but growth in Nainital between 1993-94 and 1997-98 was negative.

Graph 2(a)

NDDP (Rs. Cr.) in Uttarakhand at Current Price (1997-98)

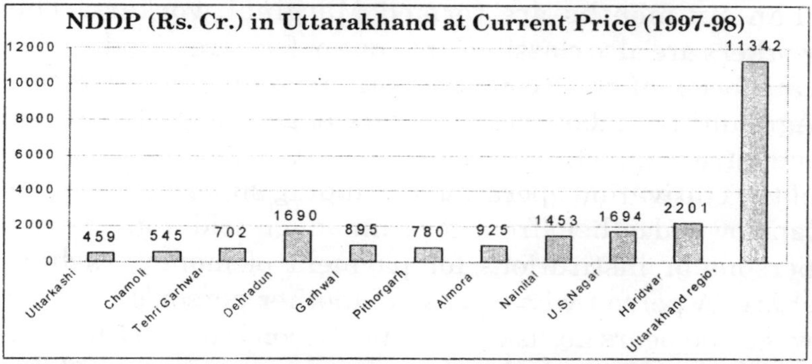

Source: State Planning Department, Government of Uttarakhand.

Graph 2(b)

NDDP Per Capita (Rs.) at Current Prices 1997-98

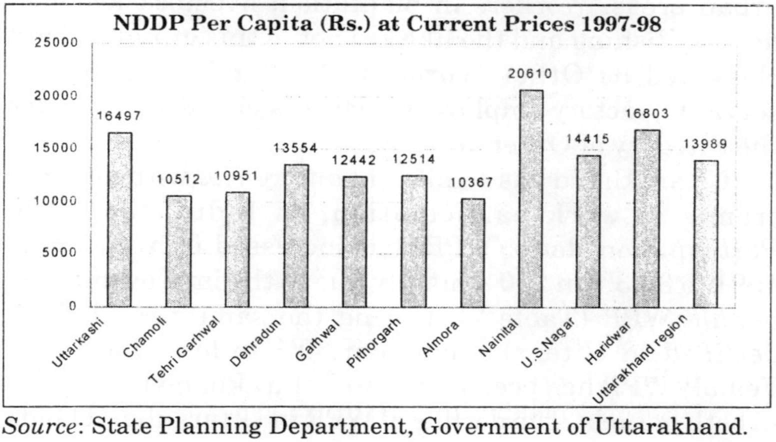

Source: State Planning Department, Government of Uttarakhand.

WORK PARTICIPATION, OCCUPATION AND EMPLOYMENT

A person is categorised as a worker if he or she has participated in any economically productive activity any time during the reference period, which is one year. The Work Participation Ratio (or WPR) is defined as the percentage of workers in the total population. Further, the workers are categorised as Main workers and Marginal workers. A Main worker has worked for six months or more during the last year while those who worked less than six months are termed Marginal workers. The workers are also classified into one of four broad industrial categories of the economic activity namely Cultivator, Agricultural labourers, Workers engaged in Household industries and Other workers. Cultivators engage in any of the cultivation operations including supervision in the land owned or held from government or held from private persons or institutions for payment of money, cash or share. A person who works on another person's land for wage and bears no risk in the cultivation is an agricultural labourer. Household industries are conducted by household member/members at home or within village in rural areas and only within the precincts of the house in urban areas. Workers in plantation, livestock keeping, forestry fishing and the like are not in this group and are classified as Other Workers. Similarly, government servants, factory employees, teachers etc. also fall under the category of Other Workers.

Uttarakhand has significant differences with all India trends in work participation. In India, the Work Participation Ratio (WPR) has increased from 37.5% in 1991 to 39.3% in 2001, mainly due to the improvement of female WPR (Table 2). During the same period WPR declined in Uttarakhand from 39% to less than 37%. Female WPR has been higher in Uttarakhand than India in both periods. The decline of WPR in Uttarakhand holds for both male and female workers. Compared to this, female WPR has increased impressively for the country. In Uttarakhand, a matter of concern is the increase in the share of marginal workers from 4.8 to 9.6% of population. As a result, the share of main workers is less than the national levels but that of marginal workers is more. The increase in the marginal workforce, which is also noted at the national level, could indicate increasing casualisation of labour due to lack of opportunities or it could mean a preference for flexibility in work conditions. Between 1991 and 2001 shares of both non-workers and marginal workers increased in the state, especially for females, suggesting contraction and casualisation of employment.

Table 2
Work Participation Rates:
India and Uttarakhand (% Population)

	Total	*Male*	*Female*	*Main*	*Marginal*
India					
1991	37.5	51.6	22.3	34.1	3.4
2001	39.3	51.9	25.7	30.5	8.7
Uttarakhand					
1991	39.9	48.8	30.5	35.2	4.8
2001	36.9	46.4	27.1	27.4	9.6

Source: Census of India, 2001.

Across districts, Bageshwar and Almora have high WPR followed by Almora and Uttarkashi. While the hill districts have high WPR, developed plain districts like Haridwar, Dehradun, Udham Singh Nagar and Nainital have lower WPR, for both main and marginal workers (Table 3). This may be due to the better quality of life in the plains that allows time for other pursuits like education. High female WPR is a hallmark of the hill districts. Female WPR is more than male WPR in Almora and Bageshwar and exceeds 40% in most hilly districts (Graph 3). Marginal workers have a larger share in the rural sector.

Table 3
Total Workers, Main Workers, Marginal Workers (% Population) District-wise, 2001

District	*Rural*			*Urban*			*Total*
	Main	*Marginal*	*Total*	*Main*	*Marginal*	*Total*	*Total*
Uttarakhand	27.77	11.86	39.63	26.29	2.80	29.09	36.94
Bageshwar	34.63	13.56	48.19	28.76	2.86	31.62	47.67
Almora	32.88	14.99	47.87	30.46	1.85	32.31	46.52
Uttarkashi	39.53	7.54	47.07	31.72	1.59	33.31	45.99
Rudraprayag	32.45	11.87	44.32	49.03	2.76	51.79	44.41
Tehri Garhwal	29.32	15.15	44.47	35.83	2.80	38.63	43.89
Chamoli	25.37	19.24	44.61	30.68	4.44	35.12	43.34
Pithorgarh	27.30	17.79	45.10	23.37	4.35	27.72	42.99
Champawat	24.96	17.11	42.07	25.51	3.60	29.11	40.18
Garhwal	24.52	15.85	40.37	25.96	2.24	28.20	38.79
Nainital	31.47	10.44	41.91	31.47	10.44	41.91	36.70
Udham Singh Nagar	24.19	9.38	33.57	24.22	4.18	28.40	31.88
Dehradun	25.73	7.65	33.38	26.79	2.45	29.24	31.20
Haridwar	23.91	6.16	30.07	25.90	2.35	28.25	29.51

Note: The districts are arranged by total WPR.
Source: Census of India, 2001.

Graph 3
Work Participation Rates by Districts

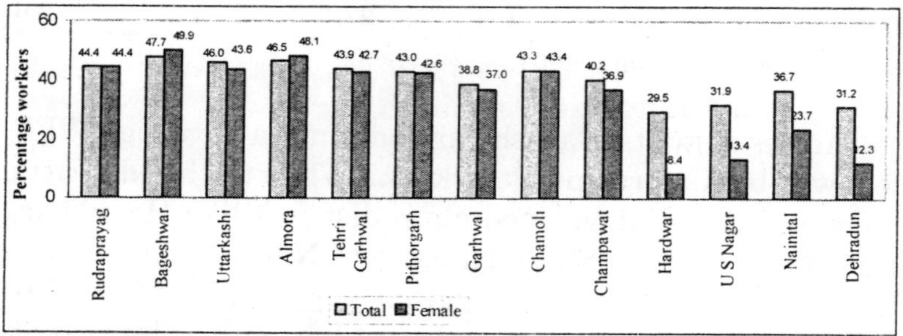

Source: Census of India, 2001.

Disaggregating the workforce by occupation, Cultivators are found to be the largest group in rural areas and Other Workers are the largest group in urban Uttarakhand. However, this occupational concentration in agriculture (Table 4) is coming down. In the rural sector, the share of workforce occupied as Cultivators declined from 66% to 62% but that of Agricultural Labours also saw only a small decline. The shares of household industry and Other Workers increased in both rural and urban areas. The share of Cultivators in the workforce is high and mostly above 70% in the rural sector of the hilly and

Table 4
Diversification of Occupational Pattern (%Workers)

			Category of Workers			
State	*Sector*	*Census Year*	*Cultivators*	*Agricultural Laborers*	*Other Workers*	*Workers in Household Industry*
Uttarakhand	Total	1991	54.22	9.05	0.98	35.75
		2001	49.77	8.26	2.23	39.74
	Rural	1991	66.52	10.20	0.96	22.32
		2001	61.75	9.75	2.07	26.43
	Urban	1991	3.81	4.32	1.04	90.83
		2001	2.31	2.36	2.88	92.45

Source: Census of India, 2001.

rural districts, but it is low for the more urban and developed districts like Dehradun, Haridwar, US Nagar and Nainital. In these districts, it is the group Agricultural labour that has a greater share. Haridwar has the lowest share of cultivators but in U.S. Nagar and Haridwar agricultural labour constitute 32.8% and 26% of the workforce. Occupation in Household industry is also higher in these plain districts and in Pithorgarh. About 39% of the state's workforce and 26% of the rural workforce are in the Other Worker category but the share is highest in Dehradun (48%) and Haridwar (38%) and comparatively low in the rural areas of the hilly districts. Household industry engages less than 3% of workforce in the state. The districts Pithorgarh, Udham Singh Nagar and Haridwar have relatively higher share of workforce in household industries but mostly in the urban sector. Thus the distinction between the urbanised districts and the other districts are sharp for work participation. For obvious reasons, only a small part of the workforce in urban areas is in agricultural occupations. Other worker constitutes the lion share of urban workforce in all districts (Table 5).

Table 5
Occupation of Workforce (% Workers) Districtwise

District	*Rural*				*Urban*			
	Culti	*Agri. Lab*	*HH Ind.*	*Other worker*	*Culti*	*Agri. Lab.*	*HH Ind.*	*Other worker*
Uttarakhand	61.75	9.75	2.07	26.43	2.31	2.36	2.88	92.45
Rudraprayag	76.85	0.54	0.92	21.69	0.07	0.00	0.64	99.29
Bageshwar	76.20	3.12	1.87	18.81	2.68	0.73	2.43	94.16
Uttarkashi	79.01	2.01	1.45	17.53	9.55	0.18	0.96	89.31
Almora	79.48	1.47	1.18	17.87	1.11	0.02	1.23	97.64
Tehri Garhwal	76.43	1.31	0.89	21.37	0.42	0.04	0.46	99.08
Pithorgarh	72.94	1.26	3.62	22.18	5.95	0.13	6.69	87.23
Garhwal	73.85	1.68	1.10	23.37	1.73	0.30	1.58	96.39
Chamoli	70.35	1.41	1.70	26.54	15.29	1.12	2.79	80.80
Champawat	77.33	2.09	1.56	19.02	7.07	1.35	2.07	89.51
Haridwar	31.44	25.97	4.29	38.30	1.61	2.58	3.25	92.56
U S Nagar	40.13	32.83	2.20	24.84	4.37	8.09	5.97	81.57
Nainital	56.69	11.51	2.03	29.77	0.79	0.43	1.33	97.45
Dehradun	36.25	13.07	2.57	48.11	0.60	0.80	1.86	96.74

Note: Culti = Cultivators, Agri Lab. = Agricultural Labourers, HH Ind. = Household Industry.

Source: Census 2001.

The employment situation in the state becomes clear from Table 6. In the year 2002-03, nearly 63000 people were registered in employment exchanges of which only 3000 were given employment. The seriousness of the situation is clear from the total cumulative registration that numbers over three lakhs. In the organized sector, the private sector employs only 13% while the public sector still has a dominant role in employment generation. Women's interest in the organized labour market is growing.

Table 6
Employment Situation in Uttarakhand (2002-2003)

Employment Statistics (No.)	*Statistics*
Employment Exchanges	20
Registrations during the Year	62864
Employed during the Year	3017
No. of Unemployed Person Registered in Live Register	338717
%women in Live register*	17
Employment in Organised sector*	272987
%in Public sector*	86.5
% in Private sector*	13.5
Total State Govt. Employee	105853

Source: Government of Uttarakhand; * for 2000 source JRC 2005.

Table 7 reports some of the employment related findings of the Fourth Economic Census (1998). Majority of the enterprises are non-agricultural in nature. Over 10,000 agricultural enterprises, i.e, agro-related enterprises excluding crop production and plantation, are reported of which about half are classified as establishments that hire labour. Non-agricultural enterprises are mostly small. Own Account enterprises on the whole constitute more than 60% of the economic enterprises in the state. Agricultural enterprises are primarily located in the rural areas and about half of the non-agricultural enterprises are also in the rural areas. However, only 40% of workers are employed in the rural enterprises. Significantly, 45% of female workers and 38% of the male workers work in the rural enterprises. Women constitute 14% of the hired workers who work with honorarium on a regular basis and 12% of all workers in the rural enterprises. The shares are less in the urban enterprises. Retailing enterprises are most common in this hilly state followed by services and manufacturing. Hotels and restaurants are next in terms of importance.

Table 7a
Enterprises and Employment (1998)

Items	*Unit*	*Statistics*
Enterprises		
Agricultural	No.	10505
Own Acct. Entp. (OAE)	No.	5361
Establishments	No.	5144
Non Agricultural	No.	204993
Own Account Enterprises	No.	142620
Establishments	No.	62373
Total	No.	215498
Own Account Enterprises	No.	147981
Establishments	No.	67517
Rural Enterprises		
Agricultural	No.	10101
Own Account Enterprises	No.	5039
Establishments	No.	5062
Non Agricultural	No.	108895
Own Account Enterprises	No.	79646
Establishments	No.	29249
Total	No.	118996
Own Account Enterprises	No.	84685
Establishments	No.	34311
Persons Usually Working in Enterprises		
Rural	No.	245455
Male	No.	216562
Female	No.	28893
Urban	No.	306659
Male	No.	279641
Female	No.	27018
Total	No.	552114
Male	No.	496203
Female	No.	55911

Table 7b
Enterprises and Employment (1998)

Persons Usually Working in Enterprises on Hired Basis		
Rural	No.	127499
Male	No.	109444
Female	No.	18055
Urban	No.	197479
Male	No.	175430
Female	No.	22049
Total	No.	324978
Male	No.	284874
Female	No.	40104
Economic Classification of Non Agri. Entp.		
Mining & Quarrying	No. / (% of OAE)	58(0.31)
Manufacturing	No. / (% of OAE)	28366(0.75)
Electricity, Gas & Water Supply	No. / (% of OAE)	276(0.09)
Construction	No. / (% of OAE)	2100(0.87)
Wholesale Trade	No. / (% of OAE)	3183(0.57)
Retail Trade	No. / (% of OAE)	85513(0.84)
Hotel & Restaurant	No. / (% of OAE)	16563(0.74)
Transportation	No. / (% of OAE)	4231(0.76)
Storage and Warehousing	No. / (% of OAE)	595(0.53)
Communication	No. / (% of OAE)	2660(0.37)
Fin., Insu, Real Est. & Busi. Ser.	No. / (% of OAE)	4226(0.40)
Comm., So. & Personal Service	No. / (% of OAE)	57222(0.48)

Source of Tables 7a and 7b: Fourth Economic Census (1998)
Agricultural enterprise exclude crop cultivation.

ECONOMIC ACTIVITIES

Agriculture is the dominant sector with an estimated nine lakh families (81%) being dependent on it. The fertile soil, good rainfall, amicable climate and ample water are important advantages in the state but unfortunately, the hilly and undulated terrains in most parts of the state pose serious difficulties such as (i) fragile ecology with easy erosion of topsoil, shallow and acidic hill soil and vulnerability to landslides (ii) difficultly of irrigation-specifically well and tube well irrigation-in the sloping and uneven land (iii) high runoff of water, fertilizer and pesticides (iv) constraints on use of machines on slopes and small plots (v) rocky soil base (vi) compulsion to undertake subsistence farming etc. Upland farming has its own techniques that minimize erosion and run-offs combined with comprehensive watershed management protocol. Integration of water harvesting with forestation is given high priority (significant allocations are made for reclamation of community watershed and marginal land). Fertilizer use is low in hill agriculture leading to low productivities but the forest ecology makes organic materials (humus) relatively abundant. The organic application helps soil fertilization and enhances soil resistance to forces of nature. Organic products have now become popular due to global aversion for chemical inputs and their residues in food. The forests also help to bind soil and reduce erosion of soil. Thus, though constrained, there are many positive 'win-win' strategies emerging for hill agriculture.

The state can be categorised under four physiographic zones broadly delineated by the altitude from the sea level i.e., (a) Tropical, consisting of plains, Terai, Shivalik bills and valleys (b) Sub-tropical (c) Temperate and (d) Alpine. The varied climates offer scope of agricultural diversification and possibilities of special and exotic crops. However agriculture in Uttarakhand has been limited mostly to food crops like rice, wheat, maize, barley, coarse cereals, etc., due to the subsistence nature of farming. Food crops account for nearly 60% of the state's gross cropped area and the state produces around 1% of rice and wheat in India and a little more of potatoes and fruits. Rice, maize, wheat and barley are produced in nearly all the districts. Area under pulses and oilseeds are low at about 10,000 hectares with pulses (Urad) being grown mainly in Garhwal and Pithoragarh. Apples are the most important among fruits contributing 40% of production. Growing vegetables on hills have been found to be highly remunerative. The state is also a natural abode of herbs and 1000 plants are documented for medicinal value. The productivity of rice is low except in Dehradun, Haridwar, Nainital and Udham Singh Nagar. Dehradun and Haridwar in the plains are noted for their high quality rice. Productivity of wheat is relatively high in Dehradun, Nainital and US Nagar. Nainital leads in fruit production followed by Haridwar and Pithoragarh. A summarization of the strengths is made in Table 8. The agricultural strategy seeks to bring out the best from the given

Table 8
Highlights of Agriculture
Forests and Industries in Uttarakhand

Cereals	• Almost all districts • High quality rice in Haridwar and Dehradun • Surplus
Soybean	• New crop • Naintal Pithoragarh
Potato	• All districts, highest in Uttarkashi, Nainital, Almora
Fruits	• Most districts–highest in Nainital • Mango in Haridwar • Apple most dominant
Forest cover	• In all districts- highest in Uttarkashi
Industry unit	• All districts-highest Almora
Small scale	
Khadi and village	• All districts
Large and medium	• Dehradun, Nainital, Haridwar • Concentrated

conditions and a balance between food security needs and the market opportunities. Some of the opportunities perceived depend on diversification to high income activities and emphases on (i) promotion of off-season vegetables (ii) improvement of quality of fruits (neighboring state Himachal provides an example) (iii) upgradation of marketing facilities for fruits and vegetables and better connectivity (iv) commercial floriculture and medicinal and aromatic plants and tea (v) reap benefits of organic farming (vi) promote value added agriculture.

Forests are important natural resources with profound benefits on soil, water, climate and livelihood. They are important sources of fuel wood, fodder, biomass and other major and minor produces and are a source of tourist attraction for their grandeur and wild life. Uttarakhand has over 60% forest coverage, which imparts on it a special status in a nation with only 22% forest coverage. Forestry has always been a sector of importance in Uttarakhand. It has an extensive and varied Himalayan forest cover at different altitudes. Except Haridwar and Udham Singh Nagar, all districts have more than 40% coverage with a high coverage of nearly 90% in Uttarkashi (see Table 17). Maintenance of such coverage in the face of economic compulsions from agriculture and industry is laudable. The variety of the Himalayan forests include (i) Deodar forests (1500 m to 2000 m) that provide wood for construction (ii) Blue pine forests of Uttarkashi and chirr forests of Terai that provide good timber for cupboard and furniture (iii) Bamboo forests of Garhwal that provide livelihood to many and bind the soil (iv) Oak forests that are a source of fuel and charcoal (v) Fir and spruce at high altitudes of Garhwal and Pithoragarh that provide wood for packing cases and (vi) Sal forests that are a very good source of timber.

The Uttarakhand Forest Development Corporation is engaged in designing logging plans and conservation through sustainable forestry, enhancing efficiency and reducing wastage. Joint forest management and other innovative projects have also been taken up. On the downstream side, forestry has crucial linkages and generates considerable employment in forest-based industries dealing in furniture, crafts, matchboxes and medicines. In addition, hill people-especially women-gather non-timber products including fuel wood often with semi-commercial motives. National parks in different districts are a great tourist attraction.

Industrialization has also been influenced by the geography of the state. Difficulties in industrial development in Uttarakhand include (i) transportation problem and near-total inaccessibility of many regions (ii) the demography of sparse and scattered population imposes severe disadvantages of scale (iii) problems of procurement of raw materials from other states hindered by the topography (iv) the soil type and uneven terrain hindering construction and mechanization (v) pollution, waste disposal, wild life conservation and ecological hazards along with interactions with plains that discourage large scale production and (vi) constraints to formation and operation of markets, low profitability, risk and scale disadvantages make private investment hesitant. On the other hand, there are substantial advantages of industries coming from (a) abundance of water (b) potentials of power generation (c) hospitable climate and sunshine in many areas (d) hard-working and educated human resources and (e) a variety of raw materials available.

Given the constraints, Uttarakhand cannot bank on large-scale industrialization that has powered the development of many states. The number of large and medium industries reported up to March 1998 is 165, generating an employment of 46000. However, 140 of these units are in Dehradun and Nainital only. The district of Garhwal and Haridwar claim most of the remaining ones. Small-scale industries (SSI) and Khadi and villages units (KVI) are more pervasive throughout the state, employing an estimated total of 84000 and 25000 respectively. Employment in SSI is high in Nainital, Almora and Haridwar. The KVIs generate a paltry employment of 1000 per district, although the figure is higher in Pauri Garhwal, Pithoragarh, Dehradun and Almora. The SSI and KVIs do not show any bias against the hill districts, but the large industries are distinctly biased towards the plains and provide employment to 14000 in Dehradun, 23000 in Nainital and 7000 in Haridwar.

Urbanized development has occurred around Dehradun and Nainital, that have also got the largest share of industries in brewery, silk, sugar heavy electrical, foundry and plywood. The state government has been giving incentives (Income Tax and Excise exemptions, subsidies on Investment, transport, land, and industrial parks) for attracting investment to remote districts. Less polluting and more local resource based industries are considered more appropriate in Uttarakhand. Broadly, they are based on agro and forest wastes and products. The forest-based industries use lightwood, ringer, resin, pine needles, fiber and produce forest products such as matches paper, board, woodcarving, woolen carpets pharmaceuticals, crafts. The agro-based industries are food processing, brewery, tea, medicinal, crafts. The industrial policy promotes new industries like Information Technology, Biotechnology. Tourism also has the status of an industry in the state.

FINANCIAL AND PHYSICAL INFRASTRUCTURE

Banks are the main source of development finance in the state. In 1994-95, there were 601 public sector banks, 176

Graph 4
Banks in Districts of Uttarakhand

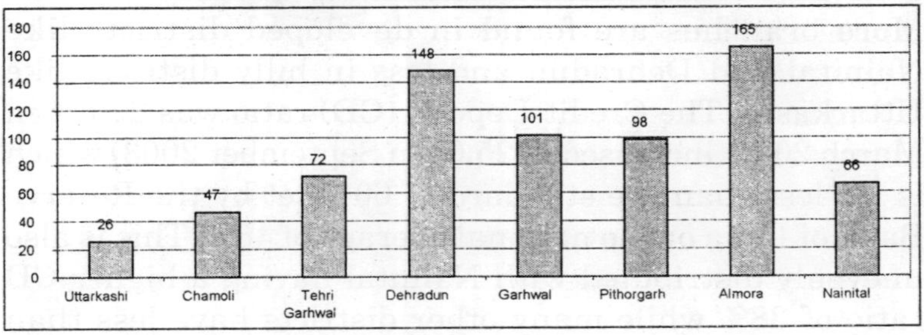

Source: 1. Statistical Dairy, Uttarakhand
2. State Planning Institute, Lucknow, UP.

regional banks, 39 non-nation-commercial banks, and a total of 816 branches. This figure has gone up to 893 in 2001 with 552 in the rural areas and another 207 in semi urban areas. Census data show that 9.5 lakh households out of the 15.9 lakh households avail of banking services and while the number is 6.7 lakh for the rural sector compared to 2.9 lakhs in the urban sector, In relative terms only a little more than half the rural households seek bank activity compared to 72% of the urban households (Graph 5).

Graph 5
Households Availing Banking Services and other Assets (in lakh)

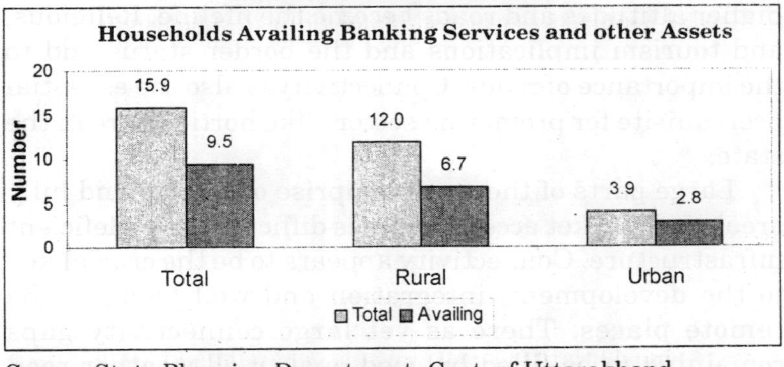

Source: State Planning Department, Govt. of Uttarakhand

The residents of 59% of the villages have to walk over a distance of more than 5 km to reach the nearest bank. More branches are found in developed districts like Nainital and Dehradun and less in hilly districts like Uttarkashi. The Credit-Deposit (CD) ratio was 22.5% in March 2001 (increased to 25.04 in September 2003) which is far less than the standard of 60% set by the Reserve Bank of India or the national average of 46%. This is also unevenly distributed with Nainital having a higher CD ratio of 38% while many other districts have less than 20%. This low rate reflects the low expectation of returns on investment in local projects and results in the outflow of resources. The CD ratio for Commercial Banks is higher in Haridwar, Nainital and highest in US Nagar. Per capita credit is low and a small fraction goes to industries. In fact, priority advances constitute 60% of credit but even for this, the distribution is uneven. Nainital, Haridwar and Dehradun receive higher per capita credit for agriculture and industry and about 12.3% of bank loans were distributed to small industries.

As far as physical infrastructure is connected, Uttarakhand has air ports at Dehradun, Nainisaine and Pant Nagar and has railway stations at urban centers like Dehradun Haridwar, Kathgodam, Kotwara and Rishikesh. Railway connections become difficult and uneconomic at higher altitudes and roads become the lifeline. Religious, and tourism implications and the border status add to the importance of roads. Connectivity is also the essential prerequisite for promoting sectors like horticulture in the state.

Large parts of the state comprise of remote and hilly areas and market access becomes difficult due to deficient infrastructure. Connectivity appears to be the crucial key to the development, integration and well being of the remote places. There as yet large connectivity gaps remaining to be filled by good quality all-weather road links. Uttarakhand has a road length of 23,673 km with about 1700 km highways and 1000 bridges. Road density per sq km is high in Dehradun, Haridwar but low in the hilly districts, which however have higher density per lakh population due to rarity of population. The densities at the state level are 33 km per 100 sq km and 248 km per lakh population (corresponding all India figures are 97 km and 309 km respectively) Sixty per cent of villages are connected, which is comparable with the national achievement. The Nirman Vibhag or the PWD maintains most of the roadways but Border Road Organization maintains some portions (Table 9). Maintenance of roads

Table 9
Infrastructure Details(2002-2003)

Transport and Communication	*Statistics*
Roads Maintained by PWD (Km)	
National Highways	536
State Highways	1138
Major District Roads	1366
Other District Roads	6544
Rural Roads	5395
L. V. Roads	2525
Roads Maintained by Local Bodies (Km)	
Motor Road District Panchayats	234
Bridal Road District Panchayats	6520
Other Local Bodies	2344
Roads Maintained by Other Departments (Km)	
Irrigation	131
Cane Development	689
Forest	3358
B. R. O.	1180
Others	178
Postal and Communication Services (No.)	
Post Offices	2717
Telegraph Offices	196
PCOs	8574
Telephone Connections	347014

Source: Uttarakhand at a Glance 2003-04.

is very important because of constant injuries coming from the slopes, water run-off and land slides. Road development also requires eco-sensitiveness towards wild life in National Parks. Table 10 summarises infrastructural information reported by CMIE. For promoting development and tourism, the state aims to upgrade roads to all weather motorable roads, provide connectivity to all villages above the population of 250 and emphasize all areas of higher altitude (860 meters). The Pradhanmantri Gram Sadak Yojana released Rs 130.6 crores in two phases incorporating 169 works on connecting village. As yet, 62% of the villages are not connected by pucca road. Finally, reliable and timely designing, optimal mixes of public-private and multi-mode transport services are the goals of the sector.

Table 10
Select infrastructure Statistics on Uttarakhand

	Energy and Infrastructure				*Banking Credit per capita*		
District	*Vill Elect*	*Post-Off*	*Tele-Conn*	*Deposit*	*Aver-age*	*Agric-ulture*	*Indus-try*
	% Village	*No./ lakh*	*No./ 100*	*No.*	*Rs.*	*Rs.*	*Rs.*
Uttarakhand							
Uttarkashi	93.8	47.4	0.19	2784	738	164	40
Chamoli	78.5	68.1	0.11	3864	540	69	50
Tehri Garhwal	74.8	42.6	0.09	4866	696	131	85
Dehradun	100.0	21.0	0.95	20575	3087	223	722
Garhwal	50.1	61.3	0.19	7702	966	154	71
Pithorgarh	71.5	64.3	0.12	4480	885	76	168
Almora	83.9	131.5	0.12	4708	691	78	96
Nainital	92.9	9.4	0.44	6704	3719	701	2118
Haridwar				8277	1885	476	756

Note: Vill Elect = Village Electrified, Post Off = Post offices, Tele Conn = Telephone Connection.

Source: CMIE-Profiles Of Districts Oct-2000.

POWER AND THE TEHRI DAM

As far as power is concerned, Uttarakhand is now considered to be a surplus state. However in reality, there is only a small surplus generated in the peak period in summer. This is a small fraction of the total potential in the state and is grossly inadequate for supporting the development of Uttarakhand. Nearly 80% of the villages are electrified and a target date of 2007 is set for complete electrification. The state expects 12% increase in generation from the Tehri project. The Tehri dam on Bhagirathi and Bhilagamga rivers is the highest dam in Asia and possibly the fifth highest in the world. It is expected to benefit Uttarkashi and Tehri Garhwal with power, irrigate 3 lakh hectares and supply water to Uttar Pradesh and Delhi. Conceived prior to 1960 and approved in1972 by the Planning Commission, the project has been delayed due to environmental activism and unresolved rehabilitation packages. A new Tehri township has been constructed to relocate the population, offices and institutions in anticipation of the submergence of the old Tehri town the headquarters of Tehri Garhwal. The project is marked by a long history of opposition with endorsement of national and international scientific bodies questioning the wisdom of building the dam. Two indefinite fasts by Sundarlal Baghuguna in 1992 and 1995 demanding independent and transparent review are landmarks of that history.

Uttarakhand Jal Vidyut Nigam (JVN) and central electricity Authority (CEA) are planning to harness the potential of the state to enhance current availability of about 700 MW by emphasizing small hydro plants with private investment. Large and medium sized plants that are environmentally sensitive are to be implemented by state run NHPC, THDC and NTPC. Hydropower export to surrounding states will generate funds for development. There are more than 17 hydro projects and some more are in the pipeline including the controversial Tehri dam that is expected to start working by June 2006. Besides these projects, UREDA- an agency dealing with renewable energy - has been helping bring electricity to homes and localities in remote places through home based solar power systems, solar fencing and small hydro projects with local participation.

RURAL DEVELOPMENT

The institution of local level governments has given rise to a great potential for rural development. Ensuring good governance through these institutions improve the chances of community development and participation. Panchayats are not new to Uttarakhand and have been working at least since 1920. Civil and criminal justice, improvement of sanitation and other common concerns of villagers were its responsibility. The legality was sanctioned immediately after independence of India but the aim of setting up representative local governments with financial powers fell short as the government of India came to assume increasing responsibility in social and economic spheres. In 1961 a 3-tier PRI was created based on the recommendations of Balwant Rai Mehta committee. The 73rd Amendment in 1992 finally recognised the PRI's constitutional status paving the way for Mahatma Gandhi's dream of Panchayats as the basic institutional form for a self-sufficient rural India.

The village panchayat came to be known as Gram Panchayat consisting of only elected members headed by a Pradhan. The size of the population served by these bodies varies considerably from less than 50 to over 10,000, as a special provision for the hill states prescribe that no minimum size of population be required. The other two tiers of governance are named Kshetra Samiti and Zilla Parishad according to 73rd Amendment provisions. These tiers consist of both elected and non-elected members including all Gram Pradhans in the block, Members of Parliament and Members of Legislative Assemblies. The elected members of the bodies elect the head of the upper tiers whereas Gram Pradhan is directly elected. The Gram Sabha (GS) is required to meet twice every year soon after harvesting of kharif and rabi crops. Its functions are (i) mobilizing voluntary labour and contribution for the community welfare programmes (ii) identifying beneficiaries for implementation of development schemes pertaining to the villages and (iii) rendering assistance in the implementation of development schemes pertaining to the village. The actual activities however depend on how much power the state governments transfers to them. The GS has been undertaking various activities including distribution of scholarship to SC/STs, minorities, handicapped and backward classes and girl students and monitoring and supervising of fair price shops under the PDS. The attempt to place primary education and teachers under the GS however did not succeed. It is felt that the PRI s are functioning mostly as agents of the Central and State Governments for implementing poverty alleviation programmes. With the new emphasis on governance and participative development, a Vikas Bhavan is planned at district level and relevant buildings at block levels with required computer, water and canteen facilities for public use.

The Panchayat has to play an important role in identifying the poor for various targeted benefits. The Ministry of Rural Development, Government of India prepares a list of households in rural areas living below poverty line based on a door-to-door survey and taking into account both income and social parameters. Total transparency of the list is to be ensured by displaying it publicly and by a possible re-evaluation by the District and Block level Panchayati Raj Institution. The Gram Sabha then has some power of shortening the list depending on the actual case. However the preparation has been in review. Meanwhile a high value of 35% of rural households has been notified as BPL. The occupational composition of BPL concentration among marginal farmers and agricultural labourers and social composition among Scheduled Castes are shown in Table 11.

Various rural development schemes are in process in Uttarakhand to help the poor. The Jawahar Rozgar Yojana (JRY) or the Pradhan Mantri Gram Sadak Yojana (PMGSY) and the Employment Assurance Scheme (EAS) have worked well. This is evident from the approach roads in villages, while more are planned under sanctioned plans. The employment generation capacity of such public works programmes is well known. The central and total plan allocation to rural development and social welfare programmes like SGRY, NOAP and NFBS are presented in Table 12 and Table 13. Such programmes not only promote income, employment and asset formation in the rural sector but also provide essential safety-nets to the poor, old and the vulnerable.

The Indira Awaas Yojana or IAY has been active in providing livable housing in villages subject to certain minimum eligibility conditions but the achievements fall far short of the targets (Table 14). The IAY is also an instrument for employment creation. Loan based concessional schemes are available for providing rural housing. Yet, a large number of households whether below the poverty line or above it does not fulfill the eligibility criteria of IAY nor possess the repayment capacity for the loan-based scheme. A scheme based partly on credit and partly on subsidy is planned under the National Housing and Habitat Policy 1998. Student scholarship schemes and pension schemes are also provided to the needy. The 20 Point programme envisaged 45-lakh man-days employment generation, which is surpassed.

Table 11
District-wise Result of the BPL Census (Data Base On 1997

District	*Rural BPL*	*Out of Total BPL Families*							
	Families %	*SC*	*ST*	*W*	*P.H.*	*S F*	*M F*	*RAs*	*Ag L*
Pauri	26.74%	9895	212	7525	226	1639	28882	4731	6876
Dehradun	34.22%	8158	6771	1916	206	3736	16303	3368	5681
Chamoli	51.69%	8314	1392	2966	624	2009	27642	1460	0
Tehri	56.53%	11796	9	6946	929	1388	56178	5730	5029
Uttarkashi	68.51%	10309	103	2595	374	4803	28731	3860	0
Rudraprayag	37.37%	4820	0	2746	303	16	15880	2572	0
Nainital	30.50%	7651	314	2218	210	1383	14241	2794	12439
Almora	36.58%	15025	38	6474	429	460	36599	4090	501
Pithoragarh	30.81%	8409	1489	4974	315	251	22312	2277	72
US Nagar	36.68%	8618	7410	2744	153	3404	9280	3955	71219
Bageshwar	41.63%	5842	73	2053	75	153	11522	1245	5370
Champawat	37.25%	3519	4	1689	86	535	9335	959	62
Haridwar	17.58%	10182	499	1988	195	5525	4746	1950	16677
Total 'Hill'	36.44%	112538	18314	46834	4125	25302	281651	38991	123926

Note: W = Women, SF = Small Farmers, MF = Marginal Farmers, RA = Rural Artisans, Ag L = Agriculture Labour

Source: *www.ua.nic.in*

Table 12
Rural Development Programs in Uttarakhand

Program	*Scheme*	*Year*	*Funds available Rs. Lakh*	*Central allocation Rs. Lakh*	*% Utilised / Achievement*	*Total Allocation Rs. Lakh*	*Aims*	*Focus Beneficiaries*
Sampoorna Grameen Rozgar Yojana	SGRYI1	2002-2003	3473	2844	62.16	-	Employment, Food security	SC, ST, Women
	SGRYII	2002-2003	3310	2126	55.74	-	Rural assets	
Jawahar Gram Samridhi Yojana	JGSY	2001-2002	3420	2228	67.02	2971.17	Employment, Food security Rural assets	SC, ST, Disabled
Swarnajayanti Gram Swarozgar Yojana	SGSY	2001-2002	-	552	76.83	736.4	Self-employment, Rural enterprises	SC, ST, Women, Handicapped, SHG

Contd...

Program	Scheme	Year	Funds available Rs. Lakh	Central allocation Rs. Lakh	% Utilised / Achievement	Total Allocation Rs. Lakh	Aims	Focus Beneficiaries
National Old-age Pension Scheme	NOAPS	2000-2001	402	-	56.69	362.03		
National Family Benefit Scheme	NFBS	2000-2001	192	-	34.93	194.18	Poverty Alleviation	SC, ST, Women, Handicapped
Indira Awaas Yojana	IAY	2002-2003	3021	-	76.05	3060.57	Rural Housing, Poverty alleviation	SC, ST

Note: The Sampoorna Grameen Rozgar Yojana (SGRY) is the premier scheme for generating casual wage employment and in its earlier incarnations it was known as the Jawahar Rozgar Yojana or the Jawahar Gram Samridhi Yojana that was then combined with the Employment Assurance Scheme (EAS) to form the SGRY in 2001. Meeting the constitutional commitment towards poor households NSAP seeks to provide a minimum assurance to the needy and unable constituted by old age, death of breadwinner and maternity. It includes the National Old Age Pension Scheme (NOAPS), National Family Benefit Scheme (NFBS), and National Maternity Benefit Scheme (NMBS). National Old Age Pension Scheme (NOAPS): Rs.75/- per month to persons over 65 years. National Family Benefit Scheme (NFBS): Rs.10, 000/- a lump sum benefit to a family below poverty in case of death of the primary breadwinner to the bereaved household.

Table 13
Allocation (Rs. Crores) to Rural Development Programmes

Rural development Program	*Year*	*Central*	*Total*
SGRY	2002-03	28	
SGRY II	2002-03	21	
JGRY	2002-03	22	30
SGSY	2002-03	5	7
NOAP	2000-01		4
NFBS	2000-01		2
IAY	2002-03		31

Source: State Planning Department, Uttarakhand.
For abbreviations see Table 12.

Table 14
Progress of 20-Point Program (30 November 2004)

District	*Employment*	*Indira Aawaas NavNirman*	*Indira Aawaas Ucchikaran*	*Indira Aawaas Ucchikaran*
	Percentage of Target achieved			
Dehradun	95%	46%	30%	64%
Rudraprayag	140%	79%	52%	50%
Haridwar	93%	54%	11%	41%
Uttarkashi	83%	52%	39%	45%
Chamoli	118%	78%	63%	60%
Pauri	63%	90%	22%	53%
Tehri	74%	66%	38%	77%
Almora	208%	49%	44%	53%
US Nagar	73%	63%	38%	57%
Champawat	135%	29%	6%	100%
Bageshwar	56%	66%	26%	40%
Pithoragarh	101%	92%	20%	43%
Nainital	105%	0%	5%	93%
Total	107%	59%	32%	57%

Source: State Planning Department, Uttarakhand.

The BPL identification also helps in conduct of PDS in the state. The 4.98 lakh BPL households that are identified are supplied by more than 6000 fair price shops in rural Uttarakhand and 1308 fair price shops in urban areas. Apart from these, BPL entitlement cards are given to the poorest in the Antodaya Anna scheme (AAY) at higher subsidies. The above poverty line (APL) cardholders are also included in the PDS but have to pay the full cost of the products. One of the difficulties in hilly states is the high cost of transport of essential goods including food to the interior regions. This causes persistence of subsistence farming despite other commercial opportunities. Farmers prefer to produce the basic foodgrains necessary for themselves and the local populace instead of depending on market. The scattered settlements and sparse population that discourage market formation compound this problem. The state can help the farmers to consider alternatives by ensuring a minimum supply of food through the public distribution system (PDS) and by creating the market infrastructure for commercial farming. In practice, however, the distribution of PDS is unsystematic. In Garhwal, US Nagar and Uttarkashi more than 40% of the villages have PDS but most villages in other districts have the fair price shops between 1 and 3 Km away from their residences. In Almora, Champawat and Dehradun, most PDS centres are more than 3 km away in Table 15. The markets as indicated by the data on mandis and sub-mandis, seem concentrated in Haridwar, Udham Singh Nagar, Dehradun and Nainital, i.e., the urbanised districts (Graph 9).

The department of Women Empowerment and Child Development deals with various schemes for the development of women and children in the state. The Integrated Child Development Services (ICDS) Programme is one of the world's most unique, community based outreach programmes for early childhood care and development. ICDS was started in 1975 in India with the aim of integrating services for the development of children up to six years with services for pregnant and lactating women. ICDS was introduced in Uttarakhand region in 1978/79. To date, there are 54 child development projects operating in the state with as many as 4243 anganwadi

Table 15
Percentage Distribution of Villages by Distance from PDS Outlets

Districts	*0 km*	*0-1 km*	*1-3 km*	*>3 km*
Almora	19.61	16.58	38.05	25.76
Bageshwar	25.93	23.37	31.86	18.84
Chamoli	28.57	23.37	30.86	17.20
Champawat	32.66	13.06	18.04	36.24
Dehradun	39.36	12.02	16.44	32.18
Garhwal	71.69	15.06	9.64	3.61
Haridwar	28.06	19.77	37.19	14.97
Nainital	27.95	21.46	25.89	24.70
Pithoragarh	37.44	16.15	28.01	18.4
Rudraprayag	38.69	22.48	27.83	11.01
TehriGarhwal	47.39	1.02	28.81	22.78
USNagar	51.07	8.38	21.19	19.36
Uttarkashi	61.27	16.68	11.35	10.74
Uttarakhand	34.90	16.34	27.57	21.20

Source: Government of Uttarakhand.

centers. The anganwadi center is the symbol of the government system, providing services closest to the disadvantaged communities at village/hamlet level. It is the focal point for converging various government programmes for young children, girls, and women from disadvantaged communities. ICDS contributes not only to the achievement of woman and child goals related to health, nutrition, and early child development, but also to other primary health care goals and the goals of universal elementary education. Broadly speaking, the objectives of ICDS are to (i) improve the nutritional and health status of children under six years of age (ii) lay the foundation for the proper psychological, physical, and social development of the child (iii) reduce the incidence of mortality, malnutrition, and school dropout (iv) provide supplementary nutrition to undernourished and malnourished children, pregnant woman, and lactating mothers (v) enhance the capability of the mother to look after the normal health and nutritional needs of the child through proper nutrition and health education and (vi) reduce the dropout rate of children between three and six years of age by providing early childhood education. To achieve the above objectives, the anganwadi centers provide an integrated package of (i) supplementary nutrition (ii) pre-school education (iii) health check-ups (iv) referral services (v) nutrition and health education and (vi) immunization.

The state government has a dominant role in uplifting the social sectors and infrastructure for the development of the state. The outlays on various related items have shown a rising trend and most notably education. This has combined with the Panchayat involvement in improving school education. However health allocation has a small share in total and has fallen from 2001-2002 to 2002-2003 (Table 16). The outlays however do not reveal the whole picture due to the lingering relation with parent state and the role of Central government. The overall Plan Outlay of the State increased from Rs. 1050 crores in 2001-2002 to Rs. 1543 crores in 2002-2003. In percentage terms, this amounts to a 46% increase in the outlay. In terms of plan expenditure, the state recorded a healthy growth of 37% over 2001-2002. Roads and power receive high priority and education too is significant.

Table 16
Change in Plan Allocation to Infrastructure and Social Sector (Rs Cr.)

Sector	*Outlay 2001-2002*	*Outlay 2002-2003*
Power	95.60	318.85(20.78)
Road Transport	159.71	170.23(11.25)
Irrigation	44.66	76.00(5.01)
Education	95.78	152.04(10)
Health	59.72	45.81(3)
Drinking Water	118.00	118.00(8)

Note: Figures in parentheses are share in total outlay (%).

In addition rural development programmes draw on the budget but shared by central and state governments with JGSY and IAY being the largest. The allocations in Rs. Crores as available are given in Table 10. 5.

DEVELOPMENT OF AGRICULTURE

Uttarakhand, like most hilly regions in India, is relatively untouched by the green revolution in any significant way. A large part of land area in the state is under forest cover and barren and uncultivable wastes take up high shares in some districts. About 14% of the area in the state is under cultivation and a meager 3% of area is devoted to other uses but wherever agriculture is practiced, land is used intensively (Table 17), so that cropping intensity is more than 1.5 in all districts. Crops cultivated are mostly food grains (Table 17) constituting more than 60% of cropped area and pulses and oilseeds contribute about 5%. Table 18 gives the area, yield and productivity of crops in the state. Except for wheat, the state yields are comparable to those at the national level. Rice, maize, sugarcane, Urd and soya bean are common kharif crops where as wheat, barley, gram, pea, massoor, rape-seed, potato and onion are grown in the rabi season.

Fragmented and scattered holdings and the resultant small size of farms are a hindrance to modernisation in agriculture. About 70% of the landholdings are less than 1 hectare and only 26% are between 1 to 4 hectares (Graph 6). The small size of the holdings and slopes reduce the scopes of scale economies in farming. Wheat and rice are the most important in the cropping pattern (Table 17) but area is also devoted to several minor crops. Cereals are emphasised in irrigated agriculture. Mono cropping is common is irrigated areas but mixed cropping is practiced in rainfed areas where millets, pulses and tubers are raised with cereals and oilseeds. Mixed cropping is a measure of risk reduction. Villages with good connectivity to markets are shifting to high value crops like Soya bean and fruits and vegetables.

Table 17
Crop Production

Crops	*Area (Hectare)*	*Production (MT)*	*Yield (Kg/ hectare)*
Rice	308433	614468	1992 (1986)
Wheat	400482	809882	2022 (2778)
Maize	38187	50035	1310 (1792)
Mandwa	142827	197575	1383
Sawan	78322	103501	1321
Oat	25995	31689	1219
Arhar	1769	1326	750 (786)
Urd	8995	3750	417
Moong	22	6	273
Gram	911	888	975 (833)
Masoor	15950	13079	820 (738)
Till	3170	649	205
Groundnut	2992	2722	910 (766)
Soyabean	3631	2522	695 (1138)
Mustard	13334	11430	857 (960)
Sunflower	1	1	1000 (538)
Sugarcane		7002000	60000 (70935)
Apple	55960	60495	1081
Pear	11873	66999	5643
Citrus	22970	86190	3752
Mango	22075	64456	2920
Others	301913	7764141	25716
Potato	20924	45460	2173
Vegetable	67281	403200	5993
Spices	5343.25	22930.69	4292
Floriculture	193.78	245.99	1269

Note: Figures in parentheses are all India yield rates. Gross Cropped Area is 1259391 Sq.Km.

Source: Directorate of Agriculture, Uttarakhand.

Agriculture is the main occupation in the state and

the scope of technology based in industrialisation in the hills is limited. Being a small state with low crop productivity, Uttarakhand contributes just 0.8% of India' food grains production and covers only 0.5% of the nation's irrigated area. Farming is done intensively in small, scattered farms on the slopes in hilly regions. Cropping intensity is 1.6, which is higher than the all India level. Measures are taken appropriately to till the slopes and to avoid soil erosion and water run off. Fertilizer consumption is a low 66 Kg per hectare compared to nearly 90 Kg in India. Irrigation potential is also limited in the state and current sources of water include wells and *rahats*. Rain fed agriculture is common.

Graph 6
Land Holding Pattern

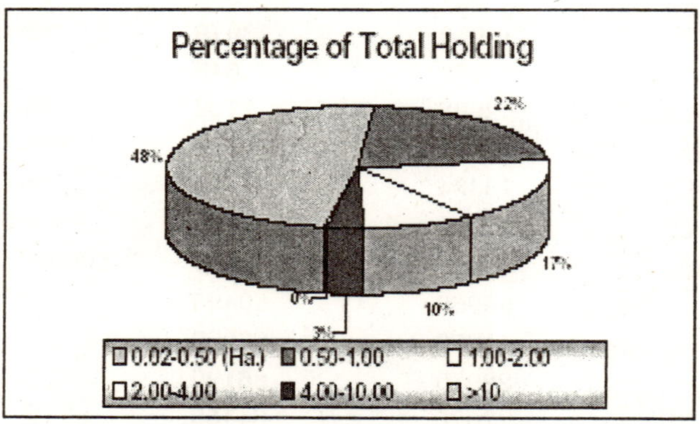

Source: Uttarakhand Rajya Vivid Soochnayen-Government of Uttrakhand.

More than 70% of the population of Uttarakhand depends on subsistence agriculture, which is based mostly on food grains. Uttarakhand is surplus in cereals, though eight districts that are mostly in the hills have a deficit. Cultivation of rice, wheat and coarse grains is widespread. About 80% of the work force in agriculture is constituted of women. The inaccessibility of the hill districts and large participation of women in agriculture are some of the reasons for the prevalence of subsistence agriculture in the state.

Table 18
Agricultural Scope

Physiography	*Soil types*	*Crops*
Irrigated lower hills (600-1200m)	Alluvial sandy soil	Rice wheat chilies peas potato radish cauliflower
Rainfed lower hills (600-1200m)	Sandy loam Residual	Finger millets Wheat maize rice
Mid hill South (1200-1700 m)	Sandy loam	Finger millets Wheat potato Tomato
Mid hill north (1200-1700m)	Brown forest soil	Rice Finger millets Wheat Potato Tomato Peas
High hills (1700-2500m)	Red to dark	Amaranth finger millet French bean potatoes peas
Very high Hills (1500-3500m)	Red to dark black clay	Amaranth finger millet French bean potatoes peas Wheat

Graph 7
Area under Different Fruits (1999-00)

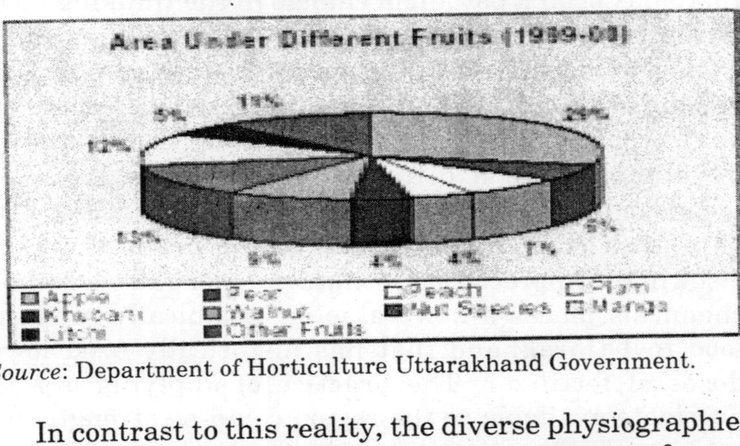

Source: Department of Horticulture Uttarakhand Government.

In contrast to this reality, the diverse physiographies in the state can potentially support a variety of crops (Table 18). Uttarakhand consists of tropical and sub-tropical zones and cool temperate and alpine zones. Besides various temperate fruits like apples and pears, tropical fruits like mangoes and citrus fruits also grow here. Currently, apples constitute 29% of the area under fruit orchards (Graph 8). Estimates suggest that the area under fruit plantations is around 0.19 million hectares and the production is nearly .58 million tones (of India's 33 million tones). Organic vegetable farming is a very promising possibility since the state can capitalise on its low level of chemical use and abundant availability of composts.

DEVELOPMENT PROSPECTS

Employment generation in Uttarakhand has always faced a constraint because of the hilly terrain and forest landscape. Agriculture has not progressed in the same way as in some of the neighbouring states due to problems of irrigation, low levels of fertilizer and resultant low productivity. Industrialisation on a larger scale is ruled out due to the terrain. The people have looked for job elsewhere and migration is high. In recent times however, there has been a paradigm change in the thinking about sustainable development and with this change, Uttarakhand finds new prospects of development. The global consciousness and recognition about keeping the environment clean has shown Uttarakhand and its development in a different light. Away from the technological ills and pollution, Uttarakhand prides itself on a pristine environment and eco-service to the world elsewhere. Appreciation of natural food raised without chemicals places a new value on organically produced food in Uttarakhand that has historically used lower doses of fertilizer. The practice of applying organic nutrients available in the region could be strengthened by knowledge and training of world organic food standards. Efficient irrigation can help to increase productivity while minimising water run off. The climate can support fruits, vegetables and flowers of different kinds. Forests are resources that hold immense value and can provide livelihood to many. The state can eschew polluting industry and build up small and agro-based industry. Most important, the state and especially the agriculture sector need development of marketing facilities and infrastructure. Graph 8 is an example of the disparity in marketing facilities between the hill and the plain states.

Graph 8
Distribution of Mandis

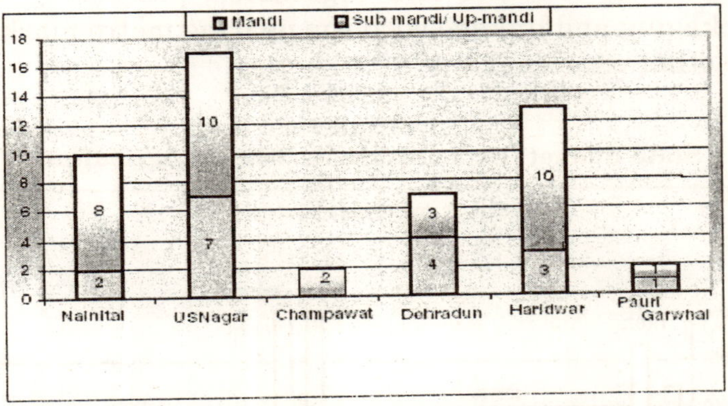

Source: Uttaranchal Krishi Utpadan Mandi Parishad, Naveen Mandi Sthal Bareilly Road, Haldwani, Nainital, 2001.

The state has highlighted the following in its vision:

1. Organic farming and effective extension system.
2. Sunrise products like Soya bean, flower and fruits.
3. Medicinal products.
4. Forest based processing like resins, rhododendron.
5. Marketing services.
6. Institutional measures like contract farming and improved credit system.

Agriculture is emphasised in the state development plan. Increased export earning and sales and growth of processing industry are possible outcomes. For this to happen there is need for human resource development and infrastructure formation along with effective extension for organic farming. The state also seeks to develop tea production especially in Pithoragarh. Linkage with pharmaceutical sector is possible by utilising the forest resources, which yield medicinal products apart from the conventional gifts like firewood, timber and juices and resin. Agro activities like bee keeping, dairy and pisciculture are also promoted. Production of fruits and vegetables, processing and packaging and linkage with the nearing metro markets are other emphases.

Graph 9
State Budget (Expenditure Rs. 000) on Agriculture

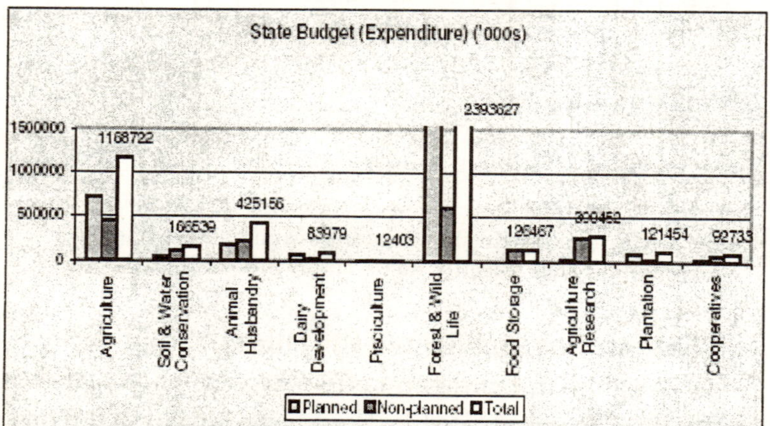

Source: GOU Varshik Vittiya Vivaran (2001-2002).

Forests are a source of fuel wood, fodder and biomass and contribute about 9% of the NSDP of the state. The forests are mostly found in Chamoli, Nainital and Uttarkashi. The state plans to improve livelihood in the state by utilising the forests in an eco-friendly way. A project on aromatic plants is in process, undertaken by the government jointly with national and international organisations for producing Lemongrass, Citronella & Basil. Development of silviculture, agro-forestry and nurseries is to be promoted through demonstrations to the locals. Eco-tourism will be promoted by building forest lodges, ropeways, and amusement parks, maintaining the national parks and through tax incentives on tourism. The Livelihood Improvement Project is another project funded internationally that is operational in Tehri Garhwal, Uttarkashi, Chamoli, Almora and Bageshwar. Several Self-help Groups and Vanpanchayats are expected to benefit from the targeted, gender sensitive and participatory work plan.

Further, the industrial planning is also based on agriculture. While the government has plans of reviving sick industries and building up IT and Biotech industries, much of the vision revolves around agro-processing and forest products. Framed against the potentialities of the state, the industrial policy focuses on sectors where Uttarakhand has inherent advantages. Tourism, Floriculture, Agro and Food processing, Handloom, khadi and village industries are some of them. Taking care not to harm the ecological balance, the state plans to take advantage of the more than 60% forest cover. There is scope to develop industries based on forest and agro-wastes such as lantana, pine needles, plant and vegetative fibers like Rambans, emphasis given to research and promotion. Encouragement to non-timber products like Bamboo, Ringal, Resin, Matches and Paper will be given to create employment. Floriculture and horticulture, which are amenable to the agro-climatic specialties of the state, will be promoted through government measures. Infrastructure, mainly transport facility and marketing services will be improved. Exports will be encouraged with

Table 19
Land-use in Uttarakhand (% of Reported Area) and Intensity of Cultivation

Districts	*Reported area Sq.Km.*	*Forest land%*	*Barren and Uncul-turable%*	*Non-Agri-cultural uses%*	*Perma-nent Pastures Grazing %*	*Trees and Groves %*	*Other Fallow land %*	*Cultur-rable waste %*	*Net area sown %*	*Crop Intensity %*
Chamoli	644395	68.19	16.00	1.76	2.12	3.43	0.16	3.23	5.11	152.44
Dehradun	304894	68.02	0.61	6.54	0.02	1.46	1.64	4.16	16.73	153.06
Garhwal	752728	59.03	4.35	2.22	5.51	7.83	2.27	5.64	13.12	152.89
Haridwar	233506	31.04	0.88	11.27	0.02	0.12	1.09	0.90	53.32	144.39
Rudraprayag	202682	43.08	28.63	3.14	3.79	6.14	0.28	5.79	9.14	161.79
Tehri Garhwal	574542	69.13	2.25	2.03	0.52	0.00	1.54	13.40	11.10	162.19
Uttarkashi	817631	88.83	2.41	0.83	1.67	0.91	0.46	1.09	3.79	157.46
Almora	585219	55.27	4.35	2.36	8.20	6.28	1.06	8.13	14.27	160.41
Bageshwar	138913	47.46	5.11	2.77	9.63	7.38	1.24	9.55	16.76	180.75
Champawat	168011	43.78	5.06	2.96	15.90	8.61	2.45	10.51	10.51	171.56
Nainital	411073	73.02	0.74	2.12	0.29	3.97	1.07	6.52	12.04	166.64
Pithoragarh	480089	55.76	3.98	2.33	12.51	6.78	1.93	8.27	8.27	181.70
Udham Singh Nagar	278678	33.45	0.40	8.88	0.01	0.37	0.89	1.31	53.83	171.48
Uttarakhand	5592361	62.56	5.27	2.97	4.09	3.88	1.20	5.80	14.02	160.61

Source: Uttarakhand at a Glance 1999-2000.

improved airlifting facility, modernising the packaging industry setting up of Agri-export Zones and with cooperation of agencies like the APEDA and NHB. Efforts are under way to establish Uttarakhand as a dominant tea producer and the tea industry can provide employment to many.

3

SOCIAL DIMENSIONS OF DEVELOPMENT

Taking off from chapter two, that gave an overall assessment of economic development and disparity in the state, this chapter focuses on the social sectors in the state. In particular, we concentrate on demography, health and education in Uttarakhand.

DEMOGRAPHY

After the state of Uttarakhand was formed from the parent state of Uttar Pradesh, the population of the new state was enumerated at 8.5 million in 2001. The demographic profile of Uttarakhand reveals a slightly different story compared to its neighbours (Table 1). Uttarakhand's population growth rate is not only lower than the national rate, but also than that of Uttar Pradesh and Haryana. The growth rate of Uttarakhand is just 1.8% per annum, marginally higher than that of Himachal, another hilly state. Also, among its neighbours, only Himachal Pradesh has a lower population density than Uttarakhand. Similarly, the overall sex ratio of the population is much more favourable to females in Uttarakhand and Himachal as compared to its neighbours in the plains. In terms of the sex ratio among children from birth to age six years, the scenario is much worse among the plains, especially in Haryana.

Table 1
Uttarakhand Population in a Comparative view
(Census 2001)

	Uttarakhand khand	*Himachal*	*Haryana*	*Uttar Pradesh*	*India*
Growth rate (exp. %p.a.)	1.8	1.6	2.5	2.3	1.9
Sex ratio	964	970	861	898	933
Sex ratio (0-6 years)	906	897	820	916	927
Density	159	109	477	689	324
Birth rate	26.1	20.5	25.9	31.4	25.9
Death rate	7.8	7.1	7.6	7.0	8.4
IMR	40	43	66	83	66
Population (Millions)	8.5	6.1	2.1	166.1	100.2

Note: Growth rate 1991-2001.

The population of the state is 8.47 million, which represents an increase of 1.4 million over its population of 7.05 million in 1991. The decadal growth rate has fallen from 24.23 per cent in 1981-1991 to 19.20 per cent between 1991 and 2001 (Graph 1).

Graph 1
Decadal Growth Rate of Population in Uttarakhand

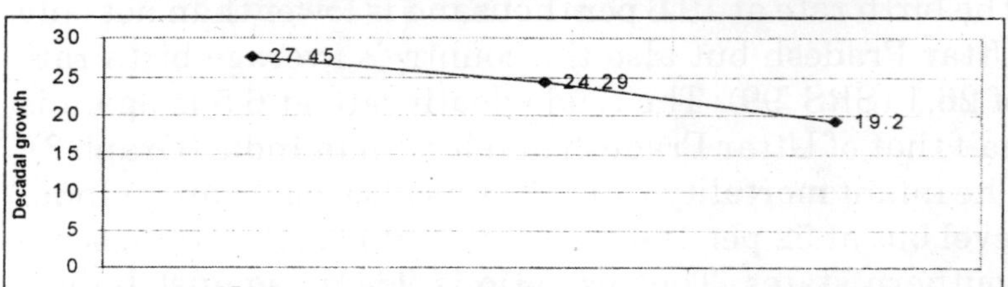

Source: Census for India-Uttarakhand.

Among the districts, Haridwar with a total population of 14,44,213, which is the highest in the state, followed by Dehradun with a population of 12,79,083 persons. In percentage terms, it is 17.03 per cent and 15.08 per cent respectively of the total population of the state. The least populated district is Champawat, contributing 2.65 per cent of the state's population. In terms of density of population, Haridwar and US Nagar lead with a density of 612 and 424 respectively as against the state's figure of 159 and the national average of 324 persons per sq. Km (Graph 2). Chamoli and Uttarkashi are most sparsely populated with a density of 48 and 37 persons per sq. Km only.

Graph 2
Population Density (2001)

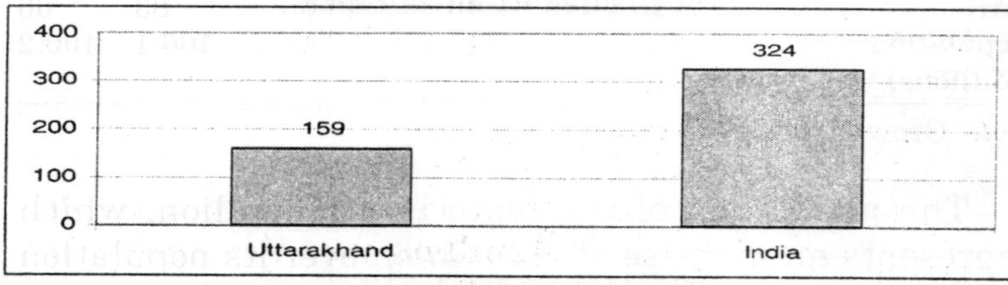

Source: Census of India, 2001(Provstonal Population totals). Uttrarkhand, Tata statistical outline of India 2000-2001, Uttarakhand Update, Joshi A. et. al.

Vital Rates

The birth rate at 19.6 per thousand is lower than not only Uttar Pradesh but also the country's average birth rate of 26.1 (SRS '99). The crude death rate at 6.5 is again is half that of Uttar Pradesh and less than India (Graph 3). The infant mortality rate (IMR) is also less than all India level but at 52 per 1000 live births it is higher than some southern states. The sex ratio is 964 as against India's 933 and has seen an increase from 936 in 1991 to 964 now, which is a positive indication of social status of women. The total fertility rate (TFR) is lower than India and is closer to Kerala. The male population comprises 43.16 lakhs while female's number 41.63 lakhs in the state. The population is largely rural with the rural population forming 76.83 per cent of the total population of the state as per the 1991 census. The rural share came down marginally to 74% in 2001 census. A larger proportion of nearly 80% of the young, belonging to age group 0-6 years live in rural areas. The rural share of this population is above 80% in nine districts, above 90% in five districts and is lower in Dehradun and Nainital (see chapter 4, Table 2).

Graph 3
Health indicators and Sex Ratio of Uttarakhand compared with Indian Average

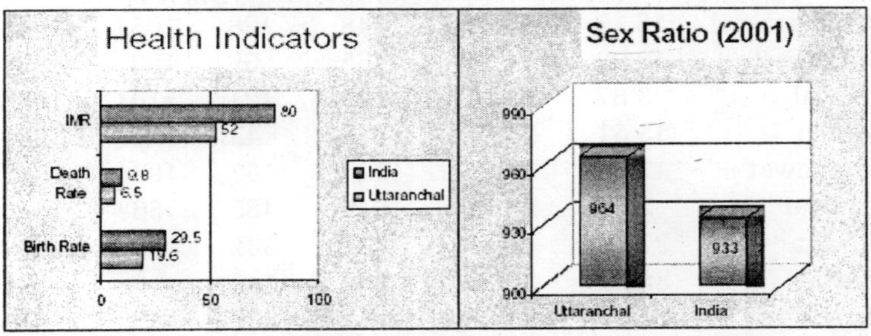

Source: Census of India 2001, Uttarakhand , Tata Statistical outline of India, 2000-2001, Uttarakhand Update, Joshi A. et. al.

The decadal population growth rate has come down in every district of Uttarakhand. Certain districts that had high rates in the previous decade (1981-91) continue to do so. US Nagar, Dehradun Champawat, Nainital and Haridwar recorded the highest growth in the earlier decade (Table 1). Four of those districts continue to hold the first four places in 1991-01. Champawat has had a remarkable decline in growth rate while Uttarkashi moved to fifth place with a small decline from 25.5% to 24.2%. Garhwal, Bageshwar and Almora have less than 10% growth and Pithoragarh barely has 11%. Garhwal, Pithoragarh, Uttarkashi and Bageshwar have thin density of population as well. The density for the whole state increased from 133 to 159 during this period.

Table 2
Population Growth, Density and Sex Ratio Districtwise

District	*Decadal Population Growth %*		*Density*		*Sex Ratio*	
	1991-2001	*1981-1991*	*2001*	*1991*	*2001*	*1991*
Uttarakhand	19.20	24.23	159	133	964	936
Rudraprayag	13.44	17.51	120	106	1117	1094
Bageshwar	9.21	14.92	108	99	1110	1055
Uttarkashi	22.72	25.54	37	30	941	918
Almora	3.14	9.43	205	198	1147	1099
Tehri Garhwal	16.15	16.59	148	128	1051	1048
Pithoragarh	10.92	14.11	65	59	1031	992
Garhwal	3.87	9.05	129	124	1104	1058
Chamoli	13.51	21.97	48	43	1017	982
Champawat	17.56	34.22	126	107	1024	945
Haridwar	26.3	28.44	612	485	868	846
US Nagar	27.79	44.46	424	332	902	863
Nainital	32.88	30.01	198	149	906	881
Dehradun	24.71	34.66	414	332	893	843

Note: Density-Persons/ Sq. km., Sex ratio-No. of females per 1000 males.

Sex Ratio

The sex ratio has improved in all districts (936 to 964 for the state), perhaps indicative of the attention and care for the girl child. The number of districts with more females than males increased from 5 in 1991 to 8 in 2001. The inter district variation is acute, especially between a plain district like Haridwar and a hill district like Chamoli. The behaviour of sex ratio is generally explained by the possibility that females enjoy a better social status in the hills. The Census findings could also (to an extent) account for the high out-migration of male members in hills. On the other hand, within the 1 to 6 age group, the ratio is not in favour of the female sex, in either of the two sectors, a finding that may support the out-migration hypothesis (see Table 2). This conjecture has led some analysts to hypothesise that women who constitute the ' prime movers and backbone' of the economy in the hill state are only tied up in an 'oppressive patriarchal society' where their 'labour', 'fertility', 'sexuality' and 'mobility' are 'controlled by men'. Further questions on the use of medical technology for sex determination arise. Table 3, on the effect of falling birth and death rates shows that little has change in demographic composition in this period.

Table 3
Population (%) by Age-groups

Age- group	*1991*	*2001*
0-9	25.87	23.5
10-14	12.35	12.9
15-29	26.25	-
15-59	54.15	55.7
60 above	6.93	7.7

Source: Census of India (*www.censusindia.net*).

Literacy is an important factor associated with the sex ratio. Barring Haridwar, U S Nagar, Nainital, Dehradun and Uttarkashi other districts have sex ratio in favour of females in 2001. Haridwar, which has relatively low literacy, also has the lowest sex ratio. Rural Haridwar also shows the lowest ratio in the 0-6 years age group.

Fertility and Population

The growth rate of population is a result of the birth rate and death rate. The vital rates, i.e., crude birth rate (CBR) and fertility rate have been estimated by demographers based on Sample Registration System (SRS). Over the years both have fallen. However, the decline in mortality rates in Uttarakhand districts have offset the decline in fertility rates. The state seems to be passing through the last phase of fertility transition and the decline in birth rate is faster than the decline in mortality rate.

Guilmoto and Rajan (2002) used a 'reverse survival technique' to estimate Fertility rates (Table 4). By this technique, Dehradun again has the lowest TFR of 2.6 and only Champawat, Haridwar and US Nagar have higher than state level TFR. The CBR is higher in Haridwar, U S Nagar, Champawat and Uttarkashi and is lowest in Garhwal and Almora. But Dehradun has the lowest CBR.

Table 4
Estimates of Birth Rate and Total Fertility Rate for Districts of Uttarakhand in 2001

Districts	*Crude Birth Rate 2001*	*Total Fertility Rate 2001*	*Infant Mortality Rate 1991*	*Child Mortality Rate (1991)*
Uttarakhand	26.1	3.6	–	–
Rudraprayag	24.9	3.2	–	–
Bageshwar	25.7	3.3	–	–
Uttarkashi	28.5	3.6	98	140
Almora	23.5	3.0	63	80
Tehri Garhwal	26.0	3.2	73	97
Pithorgarh	24.5	3.1	77	103
Garhwal	21.6	2.8	48	70
Chamoli	23.7	3.0	66	84
Champawat	29.1	3.8	–	–
Haridwar	29.6	4.1	73	97
Udham Singh Nagar	29.6	3.9	–	–
Nainital	25.0	3.3	85	117
Dehradun	20.9	2.6	59	73

Source: Irudaya Rajan, 2002.

To sum up, the main trends in the demographic sector are Table 5 (i) Vital rates CBR, CDR, IMR and TFR indicate better performance of Uttarakhand compared to all India (ii) Population growth rate is falling and may be approaching replacement rate (iii) CBR, CDR and IMR are higher in rural sector and natural growth rate is slightly higher (iv) Sectoral difference in male death rate is high (v) Sex ratio of population is above the all India

Graph 4
Vital Estimates of CBR and TFR

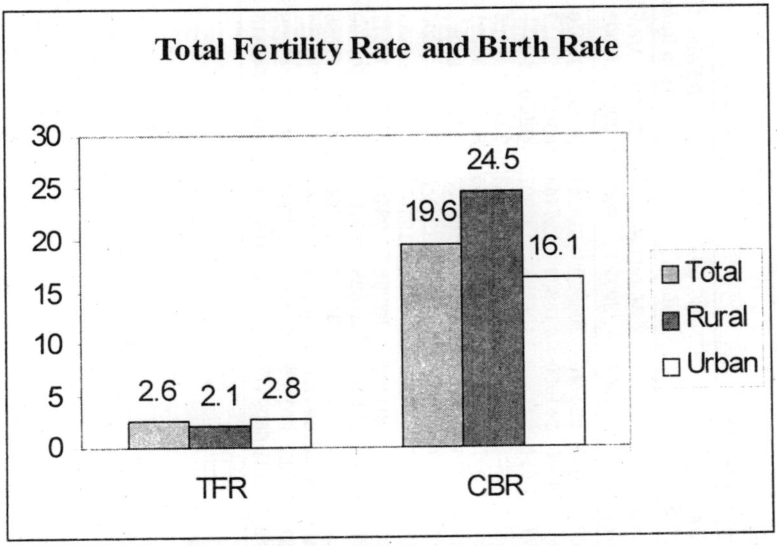

Sources: SRS, 1999, 2000 and NFHS-2, 1998-99.

level and often more than 1000 in the hilly and rural districts, partly reflective of out-migration from these areas (vi) Sex ratio in 1-6 years age group is not favourable to females in any parts of the state, but the ratio is more adverse in urban areas (the only exception being Haridwar) (vi) There is little change in the demographic composition with a slight fall in proportion of younger children (fall in birth rate), little increase in senior population (fall in death rate) and increase in working age group 15-59 and children (10-14).

HEALTH

Living a healthy life is a basic right of the people and the prevention of diseases is a responsibility of the civil administration. A clean environment, provision of safe drinking water and sewerage and inoculation are some of

Table 5
Population Characteristics

District	*All Ages Both Sectors*				*0- 6 Years Age Group Both Sectors*			*All Ages Rural*			*0-6 Years Age Group Rural*		
	Total 1991	*Total 2001*	*Male 2001*	*Female 2001*	*Total 2001*	*Male 2001*	*Female 2001*	*Total 2001*	*Male 2001*	*Female 2001*	*Total 2001*	*Male 2001*	*Female 2001*
Rudraprayag	200515	227461	107425	120036	35520	18460	17060	224740	105539	119201	35238	18310	16928
Bageshwar	228407	249453	118202	131251	40678	20980	19698	241650	113896	127754	39625	20417	19208
Uttarkashi	239709	294179	151599	142580	48591	24977	23614	271255	138328	132927	45920	23478	22442
Almora	611273	630446	293576	336870	95914	49790	46124	576497	263114	313383	90592	46965	43627
Tehri Garhwal	520556	604608	294842	309766	96159	49792	46367	546133	259078	287055	89482	46221	43261
Pithorgarh	416647	462149	227592	234557	70169	36914	33255	406025	197517	208508	63341	33082	30259
Garhwal	670859	696851	331138	365713	98791	51307	47484	606629	281581	325048	88434	45690	42744
Chamoli	325247	369198	183033	186165	54667	28258	26409	319613	154461	165152	49002	25233	23769
Champawat	190929	224461	110916	113545	39350	20225	19125	191727	93238	98489	34478	17577	16901
Haridwar	1143458	1444213	773173	671040	254207	137235	116972	998550	531528	467022	196925	106429	90496
US Nagar	966054	1234548	649020	585528	213134	111451	101683	831407	434162	397245	149225	77588	71637
Nainital	574150	762912	400336	362576	109441	57346	52095	493126	256642	236484	74466	38817	35649
Dehradun	1025679	1279083	675549	603534	162772	85537	77235	601965	314296	287669	90097	47008	43089
Uttarakhand	7113483	8479562	4316401	4163161	1319393	692272	627121	6309317	3143380	3165937	1046825	546815	500010

Source: Census 2001 (Provisional Population totals series-6).

the means of achieving this goal. In general there is also an association between the quality of life and the health of the people. Secondly, health infrastructure of the state is important for preventive diagnostic and curative facilities.

Even now a very large part of the population, especially in the rural areas, depends on sources like rivers and lakes for water that are likely to be unhygienic and at the best on hand-pumps which are common. The reach of piped water is limited. A very large part of rural households have no toilet facility. The Health Policy in India emphasizes mother and child health through various methods. The lowering of infant mortality rate goes hand to hand with population control. Infant and child mortality are two indicators of health. Effort to promote child survival is important. Analysis of NFHS-2 data (Workshop Proceeding, Reproductive child health and population policy issues in Uttarakhand, 2002) showed that antenatal care of pregnant women is one way of doing this. In Uttarakhand, mothers of only 44% of children received such check ups, which is lower than all India average. A majority of births take place at home with about 82% of rural households and 56% of urban households still have deliveries at home. Immunization against common childhood diseases has been an integral component of mother and health services in India since adoption of the primary health care approach in 1978 reinforced by the declaration of the Health Policy in 1983. The Government of India launched the immunization programme to protect children against diphtheria, pertusis, tetanus and typhoid. Vaccination against polio and tuberculosis were added. NFHS-2 survey indicates that 41% of children aged 12-23 months were fully immunized which is equivalent to the all India level. About 12% were not immunized (Graph 5). District level data available from Rapid Household survey 1998-99 showed variations. The proportion of fully

Graph 5
Immunization (12-23 months) NFHS-2

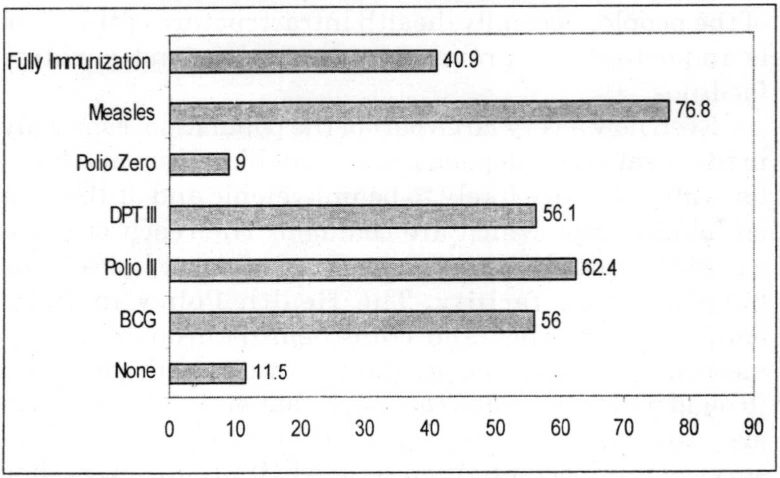

Sources: National Family Health Survey, India, 1998-1999.

immunized children varied from 48% in Haridwar to a maximum of 83% in Nainital. Uttarkashi and US Nagar have low rates (see chapter 4, Table 9). BCG immunization and DPT coverage are also low in Haridwar and Uttarkashi and are high in Nainital and Pithoragarh. With rural urban categorization not available the district wise distribution does not indicate any rural dimension.

Nutrition of children and women who are said to suffer neglect is important. Based on NFHS-2 survey data, it is seen that 42% of under 3 years children were under-weight (low weight for age), 47% stunted (low height for age) and 8% wasted (low weight for height). Malnutrition is higher in rural areas, affects girls more and children from poorer households. About one third of the women are also found mal-nourished and the prevalence is more among women in rural areas. A little less than half the women have anemia.

Family planning is integral in the health programme of the country. Facilities have been created in Uttarakhand but substantial degree of unmet need has been identified. About 40% of the relevant women use modern methods, of which sterilization is most common. Ignorance and risk of methods cause deterrence. Table 6 provides various statistics related to health status in Uttarakhand drawn from RCH survey data.

Table 6
The Challenges before the State Regarding Maternal and Child Health

Indicators	*Status in Uttarakhand*
Under five mortality rate	56.4
Percentage of births within 24 months of previous	24.8
Antenatal check up from a health professional	43.5
Two or more tetanus toxoid injections	54.2
Iron and folic acid Tablets or Syrup	38.6
Assistance from a doctor	24.9
Assistance from a traditional birth attendant	45.8
Percentage of children who receive all the vaccination	40.9
Percentage of women with anemia	45.2
Percentage of children aged 6-35 months with anaemia	76.6
Percentage of children chronically undernourished (stunted)	46.5
Percentage of children acutely undernourished (wasted)	7.3
Percentage of children underweight	41.4

Source: DLHS- RCH Round-2, 2002.

In Table 7 Uttarakhand is found to have performed significantly better than the parent state of Uttar Pradesh in most indicators. In comparison to all India figures, its performance is better in literacy, death rate and infant mortality rate and comparable in terms of other measures. However the state faces challenges with respect to women's reproductive health aspects even in comparison to the national scenario.

Table 7
Comparative Statement of Uttarakhand State's Health Indicators With India and Uttar Pradesh (2001)

Indicator	*Uttarakhand*	*U.P.*	*India*
Decadal Growth	19.2%	25.8	21.34%
Literacy Rate	72.28	57.36	65.38
(a) Male	84.01	70.23	75.85
(b) Female	60.26	42.98	54.16
Crude Birth Rate	26.0	32.80	26.0
Crude Death Rate	6.50	10.5	8.7
Infant Mortality Rate	52.00	84.00	70.0
Total Fertility Rate	3.06	3.99	2.85
Sex Ratio	964	879	933
Couple Protection Rate	43.1	38.2	44.0
Complete Immunized Children	40.9	21.2%	42.0%
Safe Delivery	51.2	20.8	40.2
Unmet Need for Family Planning	21.0	25.1	15.8
Women with Children 3 and above	51.1	59.9	45.8
RTI among Women	41.2	38.1	34.0
Institutional Delivery	18.1	16.2	34.0

Source: Department of health and Family Welfare, Government of Uttarakhand.

Health Infrastructure

The curative aspect of health is equally important for a healthy life. Unfortunately data on health facility is not available from the Directorate of Health's information. RCH data gives some idea that is utilized here. The prevalence of common and specific diseases calls for health facilities such as government hospital or health centres. Infectious diseases also call for specialized institutions. In Uttarakhand, leprosy is prevalent to some extent and the incidence is higher in Uttarkashi. TB prevalence is also relatively high in Haridwar and Nainital (Table 8).

Table 8
Prevalence of Leprosy and Tuberculosis

District	*Leprosy (per 10,000)*	*TB (per lakh per annum)*
Uttarkashi	8.87	148
Almora	1.39	122
Tehri Garhwal	2.89	110
Pithorgarh	1.98	111
Pauri Garhwal	1.24	141
Chamoli	3.17	193
Nainital	3.22	295
Dehradun	3.16	369

Source: DLHS-RCH Round-2, 2002.

The health infrastructure in Uttarakhand including private institutions has 28 different types of institutions spanning the two sectors. Some offer services to men and women and some exclusively to women. Some are specialised services to control some particular diseases. The sub-centres, designed to serve only 3000 people in hill regions, serve more population now with the increase in population. In general health has remained a public service. The government hospitals provide a high share of beds for patients in nearly all districts while private presence is visible only in Haridwar, Dehradun and US Nagar (Table 9).

The dispensaries have one medical officer with allopathic or ayurvedic qualification. The State Allopathic Dispensaries (SAD) is located in both rural and urban areas. There are 173 Additional Primary Health Centres (APHC) with one medical sanctioned position each, 23 Community Health Centres (CHC) and 84 Block Community Health Centres (BPHC). Some districts like Tehri Garhwal have no CHCs. The qualities are not uniform. There are also 38 rural female hospitals (many in Pauri Garhwal) and 15 combined hospitals. Employee state Insurance (ESI) dispensaries serve employees of organised sector. Of the four such centers in the state

Table 9
Public and Private Sector Allopathic Hospital Beds

	Beds / '000 Population	*Government %*	*Private %*
Rudraprayag	0.82	100.00	0.00
Bageshwar	0.47	100.00	0.00
Uttarkashi	1.01	96.62	3.38
Almora	1.44	88.40	11.60
Tehri Garhwal	0.61	82.48	17.52
Pithorgarh	1.34	83.55	16.45
Pauri Garhwal	1.42	95.54	4.46
Chamoli	1.11	100.00	0.00
Champawat	0.64	87.50	12.50
Hardwar	0.97	33.29	66.71
Udham Singh Nagar	0.45	79.78	20.22
Nainital	1.75	94.37	5.63
Dehradun	1.71	46.80	53.20

Source: DLHS- RCH Round-2, 2002.

three are located in Dehradun. The Central government hospitals are captive hospitals catering to employees of big Public Sector Units. All districts except Tehri Garhwal, Chamoli and Bageshwar have voluntary hospitals run by charitable trusts in rural and urban sectors. Five districts have infectious disease hospitals (Table 11) including 3 Leprosy hospitals in Dehradun, Tehri Garhwal and Pithoragarh, two TB sanatoriums in Nainital and other TB and Leprosy centres. Besides a number of Ayurvedic dispensaries serve people (Table 12). A total of 6379 positions are sanctioned but these include 474 who are likely to move to Uttar Pradesh leaving one third of the total positions vacant. There will be an acute shortage of medical officers especially male. Deflated by population even the sanctioned positions come to more than 5000 population per doctor compared to an ideal number of 1000. Similarly more than three-fourths of laboratory technicians, 60% X-Ray technicians' positions are vacant (Table 10).

Table 10
Number of Sanctioned Positions, Staff in Position and Vacant Positions in Uttarakhand, 2002

Name of the Position	*Sanctioned Position*	*In Position Uttara-khand*	*Population / Sanctioned Position*	*% Vacant*
MOs-A Grade	295	106	28744.28	64.1
MOs-B Grade *(Male)*	1187	476	7143.69	59.9
MOs-B Grade *(Female)*	147	92	57684.10	37.4
Dentists	51	23	166265.92	54.9
Sisters	158	116	53668.11	26.6
Upcharikas	571	431	14850.37	24.5
Laboratory Technicians	263	62	32241.68	76.4
X-ray Technicians	72	31	117771.69	56.9
Health Supervisions *(M)*	345	170	24578.44	50.7
Health Supervisions *(F)*	348	215	24366.56	38.2
Female workers	1933	1902	4386.74	1.6
Male workers	855	656	9917.62	23.3
Drug Inspectors	5	1	1695912.40	80.0
Inspectors	149	22	56909.81	85.2
Total	6379	4303	2076	32.5

Note: Sanctioned positions include positions to be moved to Uttar Pradesh. Source: DLHS- RCH Round-2, 2002

There is an urgent need to improve health positions to make adequate health services available. The government supplies 72% of the allopathic hospital beds in the state, 60% of which is in the districts Garhwal, Almora, Dehradun and Nainital. Dehradun, Nainital and Haridwar. The urbanised districts have more than 60% of the beds in both public and private sectors. Private beds are mostly concentrated in Dehradun and Haridwar. Comparing the number of beds per thousand people, Nainital and Haridwar again enjoy advantage but the number is also favourable for hill districts like Pithoragarh and Almora. Some of the features of the health infrastructure in the state that reveal a systemic failure include (i) a fledgling Directorate with many posts lying

Table 11
Hospital and Centres for Special Diseases

	Tuberculosis hospital clinics	*Leprosy hospitals*	*Urban Leprosy Centres*	*Infectious Disease Hospitals*
Uttarkashi	1	0	1	–
Almora	1	–	1	–
Tehri Garhwal	1	1	1	–
Pithorgarh	2	1	1	1
Pauri Garhwal	1	–	1	–
Chamoli	2	–	1	1
Champawat	–	–	–	–
Hardwar	1	–	–	1
Udham Singh Nagar	–	–	1	–
Nainital	3	–	1	–
Dehradun	2	1	1	2
Total	14	3	9	5

Sources: DLHS-RCH,1998-99.

Table 12
Public Health and Family Welfare (2002-2003)

State Allopathic Hospitals and Dispensary (No.)	*Statistics*
District Level Hospital	19
P.H.C./Additional P.H.C.	228
Community Health Centre	36
State Allopathic Hospitals	325
Joint/ Women Hospital	47
Tehsil/ Distt. Level Pregnancy Centre	24
Health Post	9
Tuberculosis Hospital/Clinic	18
Leprosy	3
Beds in Govt. Hospitals	7119
Family Welfare Services (No.)	
Women & Child Welfare Centre	2
Women & Child Welfare Sub-Centre	1525
Ayurvedic & Unani Hospital (No.)	
Ayurvedic Hospital	467
Unani Hospital	3
Homeopathic Hospital / Dispensary (No.)	66

Sources: NFHS-2,1998-99.

vacant (ii) only one health sub-centre for every ten villages (iii) no district hospitals in the three new districts of Champawat, Rudraprayag and Bageshwar (iv) only one private medical college and (v) a large proportion of sanctioned positions in the health institutions lying vacant with vacancies more acute in the remote and hilly regions. Most of the hospital beds are government given but private sector has contributed in Dehradun, Haridwar and Pithoragarh... The Integrated Child Development Service (ICDS) has worked on the health of child and woman and Anganwadis serve most villages.

EDUCATION

National policies in India have always underscored the constitutional resolve to provide quality education to all. The Directive Principles of State had envisaged free and compulsory education for children. Specifically the Supreme Court (The Unnikrishnan case 1993) declared education of children up to age 14 years as a Fundamental Right. The Operation Blackboard and the Sarva Siksha Abhijan are recent attempts in this direction. Although higher education is important and emergences of centres of excellence in universities have been simultaneous goals, emphasis is laid on school education, which has been relatively neglected for years. The curricular framework is to make education relevant and a route to life skills. It aims at complete 5 years of primary education by 2007 and 8 years elementary education by 2010. The timing of the study makes it possible to capture some of the effects of the so called Education for All (EFA) decade following the National Education Policy of 1986 and international initiatives on school education.

Educations being in the Concurrent List, the initiative of both the Central and State governments are important. Some of the instruments of universalising school education in the 1990s are:

1. Improving access by building schools within reasonable distance of a habitation, establishing primary school in small habitations and through programme in remote habitations.
2. Providing at least 2 classrooms in each primary school with toilets for boys and girls.
3. Recruitment of Teachers where necessary. Shortage of female teachers in rural areas has been problem.
4. Focus on backward areas and backward classes. The national 1986 aimed at universal enrolment of Dalit (SC) children 6-11 years age and 75% in 11-14 years age group.
5. Gender dimension to be redressed and girls encouraged to enrol and stop dropping out. Special scholarships are provided to girls.
6. Initiatives like that of providing elected management, decentralising management involving Panchayats and Local bodies and scholarships for attendance.
7. Attention to improvement of enrolment and also to retain students. The Mid-day meal is such a scheme that has encouraged school attendance while improving food security.

Literacy

The minimum measure of education is the literacy rate. In India literacy has improved from 52.2 in 1991 to 65.4% in 2001. During the same period, Uttarakhand improved from 57% to nearly 73%. Despite the constraints imposed by the geography, Uttarakhand is among the most literate states in the country. Literacy in Uttarakhand is found to be more than all India level in the period under study . The rate is however considerably lower than Kerala (91%). The rural urban gap in literacy exists as in the rest of

India, but to an even larger degree, with the urban to rural ratio of literacy rate being 1.2.

Graph 6
Literacy Rate (2001)

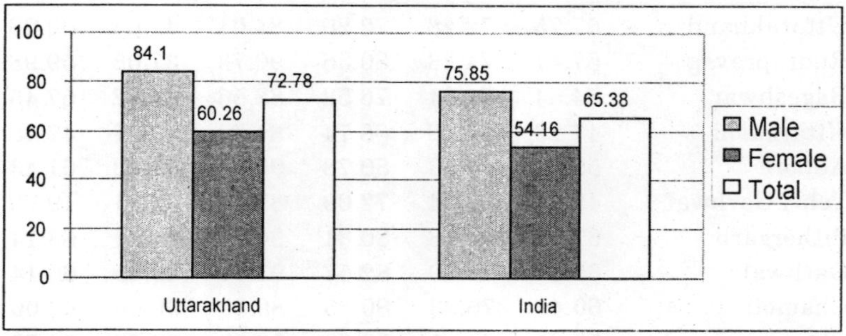

Source: Census for India-Uttarakhand

The literacy rate is 84.01 for the males while it is 60.26 per cent for the females (Graph 6) both higher than national leverages. Also, both male and female literacy rates have improved. The gender gap in literacy is high underscoring the importance of encouraging education of girls. The gender ratio of literacy rate is 1.4 for the state and 1.5 rural sectors.

The district level performances are complex. There is no distinct pattern of bias across district. Relatively developed districts like Nainital and Dehradun and hilly districts including Chamoli and Pithoragarh and Almora record high literacy rates while developed district Haridwar surprisingly has low literacy as also US Nagar and Uttarkashi. Uttarkashi, Tehri Garhwal and Dehradun recorded significant improvement in literacy rates in 2001 over 1991 (Table 13). Nainital, which has the highest literacy of 79%, had the slowest increase.

Male literacy is high (above 80%) in most districts and above 90% in Garhwal, Rudraprayag, Pithoragarh and Almora, all hilly districts. It is as yet less than 80% only

Table 13
Literacy Rates Changes by Districts, Uttarakhand

State / District	*Literacy Rate*					
	Persons		*Males*		*Females*	
	1991	*2001*	*1991*	*2001*	*1991*	*2001*
Uttarakhand	57.75	72.28	72.29	84.01	41.63	60.26
Rudraprayag	57.47	74.23	80.36	90.73	37.08	59.98
Bageshwar	54.54	71.94	76.52	88.56	34.22	57.45
Uttarkashi	47.23	66.58	68.74	84.52	23.57	47.48
Almora	59.83	74.53	80.78	90.15	41.32	61.43
Tehri Garhwal	48.46	67.04	72.09	85.62	26.31	49.76
Pithorgarh	61.38	76.48	80.31	90.57	42.41	63.14
Garhwal	65.53	77.99	82.57	91.47	49.65	66.14
Chamoli	60.40	76.23	80.85	89.89	39.66	63.00
Champawat	55.81	71.11	77.63	88.13	32.62	54.75
Haridwar	47.97	64.60	59.28	75.06	34.37	52.60
Udham Singh Nagar	49.29	65.76	60.47	76.20	36.02	54.16
Nainital	68.36	79.60	80.42	87.39	54.51	70.98
Dehradun	69.50	78.96	77.95	85.87	59.26	71.22

Source: Census of India 2001, Series-6.

in US Nagar and Haridwar. These two districts also record low female literacy compared to the state average. The same is true of Uttarkashi, Tehri Garhwal, Champawat, Bageshwar and Rudraprayag all of which have more than 80% male literacy. The gender gap appears to be wide in these cases. Female literacy rate for the state is only 60%, which is more than 20 points less than that for the male. It is above 70% only in Dehradun and Nainital and is less than 50% in Uttarkashi and Tehri Garhwal.

School Education

Although literacy rate is an outcome indicator, it is neither adequate nor indicative of the means and progress of educational diffusion. The 1990s decades saw a spur of proactive infrastructural development to spread education. NCERT's All India Education Survey (2000) makes it possible to examine the progress in school education and especially primary education information on infrastructure, access and adoption. Table 14 shows that Uttarakhand compares well with all-India and with neighbouring states, with higher (more than 100%) gross enrolment ratio (better in rural sector), lower pupil teacher ratio, better gender balance in schooling and higher growth rate of schools with respect to primary schooling.

Table 14
Primary School Comparative Statistics with Neighbouring States 2002

	Enrolment ratio		*Pupil / Teacher*		*% Increase over 1993*		*%Girls*	
	Rural	*Total*	*Rural*	*Urban*	*Rural*	*Urban*	*Rural*	*Urban*
Uttarakhand	105	104	29	27	37	62	49	46
Uttar Pradesh	88	88	61	36	48	49	36	45
Himachal	111	112	22	23	42	1	48	44
Haryana	81	78	42	35	82	111	46	45
Punjab	74	68	39	36	4	14	47	46
India	92	93	44	36	13	24	47	47

Source: NCERT, 2000.

Access and easy reach have been identified as a way to expend enrolment. This is particularly relevant in a state where transportation is not easy. Haridwar has the largest share of habitations with a school within them, so that the travelling out is not necessary. Provision of schools within or within a short distance of the habitations is an indicator of access. Although the access is good with more than 80% of habitations having a primary school within one km distance, a significant section (16%) of habitations have schools beyond One km This is as high as 25% in Champawat where female literacy is not satisfactory. With transport being a problem, the distance poses a challenge for education and especially for girls whose safety is a concern for the families. Even at the upper primary stage the access is not as good and the largest section (70%) have schools outside the habitations (but within 3 Km). Champawat once again has the largest (26%) habitations with this facility further than 3 Km (Table 15).

Table 15
Percentage of Habitations with Access to Schools District-wise

District	*Primary Stage*			*Upper Primary Stage*		
	Within habitation	*Within one km*	*Beyond one km*	*Within habitation*	*Within three km*	*Beyond three km*
Rudraprayag	42.20	44.41	13.39	16.36	75.00	8.64
Bageshwar	38.11	47.21	14.68	9.51	73.54	16.95
Uttarkashi	60.69	23.29	16.01	21.11	60.60	18.29
Almora	40.37	45.56	14.07	10.54	75.60	13.86
Tehri Garhwal	46.82	36.24	16.94	16.97	71.12	11.91
Pithorgarh	31.91	48.59	19.50	9.08	73.56	17.36
Garhwal	41.24	44.45	14.31	15.18	73.88	10.94
Chamoli	43.85	39.32	16.83	13.34	71.80	14.86
Champawat	34.79	39.83	25.38	9.63	63.61	26.76
Haridwar	86.36	8.22	5.42	24.13	52.62	23.25
U S Nagar	60.13	28.98	10.89	22.54	67.05	10.42
Nainital	44.98	40.36	14.66	17.42	73.18	9.40
Dehradun	54.13	28.68	17.18	19.70	59.74	20.56
Uttarakhand	43.87	40.20	15.92	14.42	70.92	14.66

Source: NCERT, 2000.

About 74% of rural schools and 60% of urban schools are primary schools. In the urban region the share is high in Bageshwar at 75%, and lowest at 54% in Garhwal. Considering the infrastructure, the proportion of pucca school building is lower in the rural sector (69.8%) than in the urban sector (86%). Among the districts the urban infrastructure is uniformly high but in rural areas there are disparities though there is no bias between hill and plain districts (Table 16).

Table 16
School Infrastructure District-wise (percentage)

District	Rural			Urban		
	Total Schools	Primary School	Pucca School	Total Schools	Primary School	Pucca School
Rudraprayag	786	70.99	65.01	12	58.33	89.73
Bageshwar	749	78.91	77.70	12	75.00	96.52
Uttarkashi	1015	73.79	68.37	46	58.70	85.84
Almora	1813	78.27	76.89	80	58.75	76.41
Tehri Garhwal	1950	72.41	67.28	97	57.73	85.81
Pithorgarh	1489	77.03	70.11	86	58.14	82.92
Garhwal	2416	71.48	66.06	121	53.72	81.32
Chamoli	1271	74.43	71.13	106	63.21	88.87
Champawat	627	75.92	71.61	37	56.76	79.26
Haridwar	989	78.06	74.92	400	64.75	86.42
U S Nagar	1059	72.71	69.50	349	61.60	88.64
Nainital	1329	71.33	70.35	277	60.65	86.21
Dehradun	1331	71.45	63.49	753	59.10	93.09
Uttarakhand	16824	74.10	69.80	2376	60.44	86.2

Source: NCERT, 2000.

Table 17
Performance in School Education Districtwise

District	Net enrolment ratio		% School receiving Grants (Primary)		
	Primary	Upper Primary	% SC in Primary Enrolment	Development Grant	Total Literacy Mission
Haridwar	73.4	28.8	30.3	67.7	66.0
Dehradun	51.5	21.3	24.1	72.2	71.9
Udham Singh Nagar	78.7	37.1	29.6	70.1	69.4
Nainital	35.2	20.8	30.8	84.3	83.3
Garhwal	59.1	28.9	24.5	88.5	90.4
Almora	78.9	45.3	29.1	93.5	92.9
Tehri Garhwal	108.4	74.8	17.9	72.8	68.3
Pithorgarh	75.2	53.0	32.0	87.3	85.1
Chamoli	89.3	69.7	23.5	82.1	83.3
Uttarkashi	84.8	37.5	29.6	82.0	82.5
Bageshwar	77.6	59.0	33.8	88.7	90.1
Rudraprayag	79.5	48.6	23.7	75.3	80.3
Champawat	82.8	50.6	22.8	91.3	86.1

Source: NIEPA, 2004.

Table 17 however shows that despite high enrolment, there is a distinct fall in the enrolment ratios from primary to upper primary level in all districts and the share of Scheduled Castes is between 20% and 30% at the primary level. Majority of the districts receive grants from government sources.

PART - II

RURAL URBAN DISPARITY

4

SOCIAL AND ECONOMIC DISPARITY: EVIDENCES FROM SECONDARY DATA

In this chapter, and the subsequent ones, we shall focus on the rural urban disparity in Uttarakhand. In this chapter, the analysis will be based on secondary data. The first part of the chapter deals with social disparity while the second part deals with economic disparity.

SOCIAL DISPARITY

Social disparity, as in the previous chapter, is discussed in terms of demography, quality of life, health and education.

Demography

We have seen in Chapter 3 that Uttarakhand is ahead of many of its neighbouring states in terms of demographic indicators. We will now explore the differences between the rural and urban sectors within the state of Uttarakhand, with respect to various demographic measures. The Crude Birth Rate (CBR) and the Crude Death Rate (CDR) are both higher in the rural sector than in the urban sector (Graph 1). The natural growth rate (NGR) is thus not much different between sectors and follows the same direction. The Infant Mortality Rate

(IMR), which affects the population growth rate indirectly, is however much higher in the rural sector (69) than the urban sector (26) according to Census 2001.

Graph 1
Vital Estimates of CBR, CDR, NGR, IMR, 2001

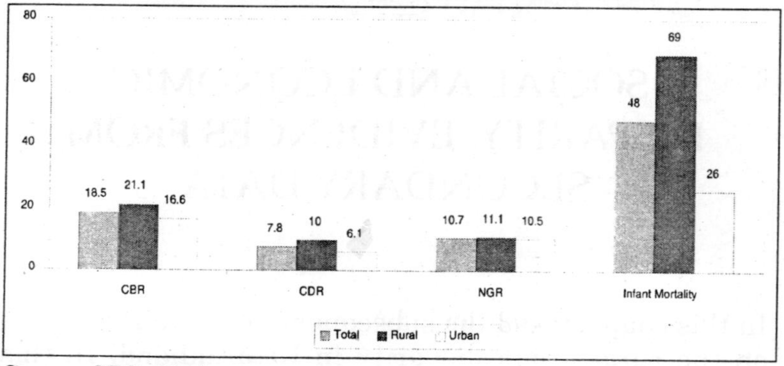

Source: SRS, 2001.

The gender dimension in the demographic indicators is also worth noting. The male death rate is higher in the rural sector (13.4) compared to the female death rate (7) as seen in Graph 2. The gender differential is much smaller in urban areas (4.4 and 4.6 for male and female respectively). Male infant mortality is 67 and 42 in rural and urban sectors. Female infant mortality at 77 is significantly higher in rural sector. Table 1 indicates the movements of the vital indicators over time. The CBR has fallen from 24.5 in 1999 to 21.1 in 2001 in the rural sector but in the urban sector the birth rate has increased marginally from 16.1 to 16.6 during the same time. The CDR during the same period has shown a similar dynamics and the increase from 3.5 to 6.1 is intriguing. The IMR has declined in both sectors though the fall is less significant in the urban sector. The directions seen in the urban sector of the state leaves scarce room for complacency.

Graph 2
Death Rates and Infant Mortality Rates by Sex and Sctors

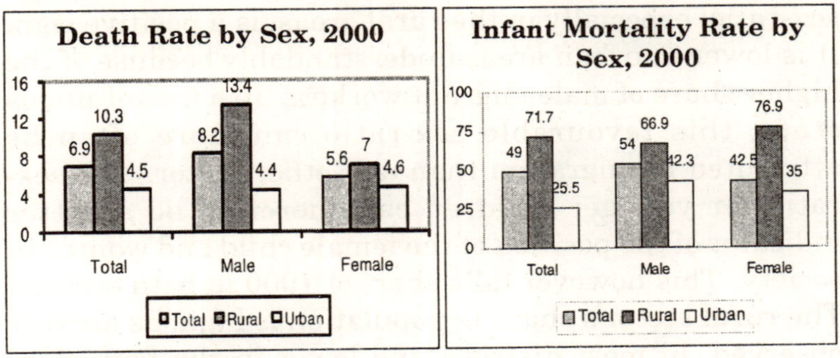

Source: Census, 2001.

Table 1
Trends of Demographic Indicators in Uttarakhand

	CBR			*CDR*			*IMR*			*NGR*		
Year	*R*	*U*	*T*	*R*	*U*	*T*	*R*	*U*	*T*	*R*	*U*	*T*
1999	24.5	16.1	19.6	10.5	3.5	6.5	75	27	52	–	–	–
2000	24.6	17.1	20.2	10.3	4.5	6.9	73	26	50	–	–	–
2001	21.1	16.6	18.5	10	6.1	7.8	69	26	48	11.1	10.5	10.7

Note:R = Rural, U = Urban, T = Total.
Source: SRS, 2001.

The importance of the rural areas for the population of the state and its gender aspects is explored through the break up of the total population and the sex ratio into those for rural and urban areas (Table 2). More than 74% of Uttarakhand's population live in the rural areas and of this population, more than half are females as evident from a sex ratio that exceeds 1000, compared to a smaller value of 850 for the urban sector. Another interesting aspect is that the rural share of the population of young children (up to 6 years of age) is very high at 79.3%, even higher than the share of the entire population from rural areas. A large majority of the state's young children live in the rural areas.

The sex ratio is generally used to assess women's position in a society and by this standard the state's high sex-ratio, especially in the rural areas, is a positive sign. It is lower in urban areas understandably because of the higher share of male migrant workers. In a mountainous state, this favourable sex-ratio can more often be attributed to migration than any other factor. The sex-ratio for younger children can therefore be a better indicator of the position of the female child and women in society. This however falls short of 1000 in both sectors. The rural sector's share in population is high, as already observed, in most districts and lower in the four plain districts. The sex ratio is also high in the hilly districts except for Uttarkashi, but interestingly, the same ratio is not favourable in either of the sectors for the 1 to 6 years age group. Such an adverse sex ratio in the younger age group needs explanation and investigation.

Quality of Life

The quality of life of people is the sum total of various aspects of their living conditions. For a particular region, it reflects the ease and comfort of day to day living, and includes the availability of sanitation, health and hygiene, as well as physical connectivity to and informational communication with the rest of the country. Quality of life is also determined by the access to social amenities and modern technology. The Census provides a fund of information on living conditions, sanitation and assets that help in comparing the rural and urban quality of life in Uttarakhand, summarised in Table 3.

Housing condition is graded into three parts i.e., good, liveable and others. Considering only good houses, there is an obvious sectoral disparity with 71% of urban and only 64% of rural households enjoying good housing condition. But when the yardstick is brought down to liveable housing, the disparity becomes minimal and both

Table 2
Population Distribution District-wise and Sex-ratios 2001

District	*0-6 years*				*All Ages*			
	Population%		*Sex ratio*		*Population%*		*Sex ratio*	
	Rural	*Urban*	*Rural*	*Urban*	*Rural*	*Urban*	*Rural*	*Urban*
Uttarakhand	79.34	20.66	914	874	74.41	25.59	1007	850
Rudraprayag	99.21	0.79	925	880	98.80	1.20	1129	443
Bageshwar	87.62	2.68	941	870	85.42	3.48	1122	812
Uttarkashi	94.50	5.50	956	782	92.21	7.79	961	727
Almora	94.45	5.55	929	884	91.44	8.56	1191	771
Tehri Garhwal	93.06	6.94	936	870	90.33	9.67	1108	635
Pithorgarh	90.27	9.73	915	782	87.86	12.14	1056	866
Garhwal	89.52	10.48	936	844	87.05	12.95	1154	821
Chamoli	89.64	10.36	942	873	86.57	13.43	1069	735
Champawat	97.41	11.98	962	840	96.87	13.12	1056	852
Haridwar	77.47	22.53	850	859	69.14	30.86	879	844
Udham Singh	70.01	29.99	923	887	67.35	32.65	915	876
Nainital	68.04	31.96	918	888	64.64	35.36	921	878
Dehradun	55.35	44.65	917	886	47.06	52.94	915	874

Source: Census 2001.

Table 3
Distribution of Households by Conditions of Houses

	% Total	*% Rural*	*% Urban*
Condition of houses			
Good	65.9	64.3	71.0
Livable	30.6	32.2	25.8
Any of the above	96.5	96.5	96.8
Roof type			
Brick	18.0	15.0	27.2
Stone	16.1	21.0	1.0
Concrete	30.7	24.6	49.3
Any of the above	64.8	60.6	77.5
Wall type			
Brick	43.0	30.1	82.3
Stone	44.3	56.6	6.9
Concrete	0.9	0.7	1.4
Any of the above	88.2	87.4	90.6
Floor type			
Brick	1.2	0.9	2.1
Stone	2.1	2.5	0.9
Cement	35.9	24.5	70.8
Mosaic, Floor Tiles	3.4	0.9	10.9
Any of the above	42.6	28.8	84.7
Type of house			
Permanent	86.3	85.1	90.0
No. of dwelling rooms			
Two rooms	32.7	32.7	32.7
Two rooms or more	72.3	74.2	67

Source: Table H-2 & Table H-3 India: Census of India 2001.

sectors seem to be equally facilitated with a high (more than 96%) proportion of households residing in liveable houses in either sector. Construction of houses differs between the sectors with concrete being most common roof material in urban sector. About 40% of rural houses and 22% of urban do not have roof made of brick, stone or concrete. Similarly larger portions of urban houses compared to rural ones, have walls and floors made of strong materials like brick, stone, concrete and cement. Nearly 11% of urban houses have paved floor of tiles or mosaic and this is negligible in the rural sector. However 74% of the rural houses have two or more number of rooms and this implies a lead over the urban sector where 67% have that privilege. Clearly, living space is more abundantly available in rural areas compared to more crowded and expensive urban living.

The structure of the house combines with other facilities to make a good living condition. Water connection is one such facility (Table 4). In the urban sector, 82% of households access drinking water within the premises of their houses. The rural households not only fall short in

Table 4
Access to Drinking Water and Sanitation

	% Total	% Rural	% Urban
Location of drinking water			
Within premises	44.8	32.7	82.1
Near premises	38.5	46.9	12.7
Away	16.7	20.4	5.2
Source of drinking water			
Tap	65.9	60.5	82.3
Hand pump	19.8	21.4	14.9
Tube well	1.0	1.1	0.6
Well	1.2	1.6	0.2
Tank, Pond, Lake	1.2	1.6	0.2
River, Canal	1.9	2.4	0.3
Spring	2.1	2.8	0.2
Any other	6.9	8.7	1.3
Bathroom facility	38.8	26.0	77.9
Type of latrine			
Pit latrine	18.7	16.1	26.7
Water closet	15.4	7.2	40.8
Other latrine	11.0	8.3	19.3
No latrine	54.8	68.4	13.1
Type of Drainage			
Closed drainage	10.4	4.5	28.4
Open drainage	37.7	30.5	59.9
No drainage	51.9	65.0	11.8

Source: Table H-8 & Table H-10 India: Census of India 2001.

this but 20% do not have a drinking water source near their houses and have to travel to fetch water, whereas this share is only 5% in urban areas. Taps are now supplying to majority of the houses in both sectors but urban houses have better access, whereas a large share (21%) of rural houses are supplied by hand pumps and other sources including tank, pond, lake, river and springs. There is a wide disparity in housing with bathroom and latrine facility, and 65% of rural houses have no drainage compared to 11% in urban areas. It remains to be said that provision of water supply and sanitation facility is an unfinished task even for the urban households but the state of the rural households in these respects is far worse.

As far as sources of lighting in their dwellings are concerned, electricity is available to only 50% of rural households, considerably less than the figure (91%) for urban households (Table 5). In rural areas, kerosene is a dominant source of energy for this purpose. Commendably, solar energy has a sizable share. As a source of fuel for other uses, firewood is still an important factor in the forested state, accounting for nearly 70% of household while cow-dung cake and bio-gas are also minor sources in rural Uttarakhand. It is noted that firewood collection becomes an important chore of rural women and cow dung is alternatively used as manure in organic based agriculture. Dependence on natural resources and commons is evident in this pattern. Penetration of LPG is only 21% in the rural sector but 71% in urban areas.

Various kinds of assets also make the life of a household more comfortable. Sometimes apart from entertainment and relaxation, they are a source of information about the wider world and enable speedy connectivity with the same, and hence contribute to higher productivity, better governance, participation and improved bargaining power. Rural households own radio or transistor more commonly but urban households are more endowed in all other assets such as television, telephone, bicycle, scooter and car (Table 6).

Table 5
Household Access to Lighting and Fuel

	% Total	*% Rural*	*% Urban*
Source of lighting			
Electricity	60.3	50.3	90.9
Kerosene	37.3	46.7	8.4
Solar energy	1.9	2.4	0.2
Other oil	0.1	0.1	0.1
any other	0.2	0.2	0.1
Source of Fuel			
Fire-wood	54.6	67.5	14.7
Crop residue	2.6	3	1.4
Cowdung cake	3.5	4.2	1.3
Coal, lignite, charcoal	0	0	0.1
Kerosene	4.4	2.4	10.6
LPG	33.5	21.3	70.9
Electricity	0.1	0.1	0.1
Bio-gas	1	1.2	0.3
Any Other	0.1	0.1	0
No cooking	0.3	0.2	0.6

Source: Table H-9 & Table H-11 India: Census of India 2001

Table 6
Households with Assets(%)

	Total	*Rural*	*Urban*
Radio, Transistor	49.7	51.4	44.5
Television	42.9	32.3	75.6
Telephone	9.9	4.4	26.7
Bicycle	30.9	25.9	46.2
Scooter, Motor cycle, Moped	11.9	6.2	29.7
Car, Jeep, Van	2.7	1.3	7.0
None of the specified assets	25.7	30.1	12.0

Source: Table H-13 India: Census of India 2001.

Table 7
Percentage Distribution of Households by Quality of Life Indicators

Housing characteristics	*Urban*	*Rural*	*Total*
Electricity			
Yes	91.7	39.3	52.6
No	8.3	60.7	47.4
Source of drinking water			
Piped	68.3	35.5	43.8
Hand pump	31.7	34.6	33.9
Well water	0.0	1.0	0.8
Surface water	0.0	27.9	20.8
Other	0.0	1.0	0.7
Time to get drinking water			
Percentage <15 minutes	96.5	62.0	70.8
Median time (minutes)	0.0	5.0	0.0
Method of drinking water purification			
Strains water by cloth	1.1	0.2	0.4
Uses alum	0.3	0.1	0.2
Uses water filter	29.6	3.3	10.0
Boils water	15.0	3.6	6.5
Uses electronic purifier	1.7	0.2	0.6
Uses other method	0.6	1.0	0.9
Does not purify water	59.2	92.0	83.7
Missing	0.0	0.1	0.1
Sanitation facility			
Flush toilet	78.8	8.0	25.9
Pit toilet/latrine	8.5	13.7	12.4
Other	0.0	0.5	0.4
No facility	12.7	77.8	61.3
Main type of fuel used for cooking			
Wood	19.0	74.2	60.2
Crop residues	0.3	0.5	0.5
Dung cakes	0.0	8.6	6.4
Kerosene	5.0	2.2	3.0
Electricity	0.3	0.0	0.1
Liquid petroleum gas	75.0	13.4	29.0
Bio-gas	0.3	0.9	0.8
Other	0.0	0.1	0.1
Type of house			
Kachha	9.5	21.0	18.1
Semi-pucca	9.5	38.1	30.8
Pucca	81.1	40.0	50.4
Missing	0.0	0.9	0.7

Source: NFHS-2, 1998-99.

In Table 8 the state of water and sanitation and the rural urban disparity are presented for the state Uttarakhand at the district level using RCH data. A comparative view reveals that the plain districts of Dehradun and Haridwar are in a better position but among the hill districts, Uttarkashi is relatively better endowed. The rural urban disparity is sharp in all cases but wider in the hill districts.

Table 8
Percentage of Households having Access to Sanitation Facilities: District-wise

Districts	*Safe drinking water*			*Toilet*		
	Rural	*Urban*	*Total*	*Rural*	*Urban*	*Total*
Uttarkashi	66.4	94.6	68.8	13.5	76.3	19.1
Almora	62.5	86.6	64.0	5.0	67.5	8.9
Tehri Garhwal	67.8	93.5	69.6	6.3	76.8	11.3
Pithorgarh	56.5	83.1	58.9	3.7	73.6	9.9
Garhwal	72.0	90.8	74.1	6.4	76.2	14.3
Chamoli	74.3	84.0	75.3	6.2	59.2	11.6
Hardwar	88.0	93.2	89.7	14.6	81.8	36.2
Nainital	77.8	94.0	83.2	16.9	71.9	35.4
Dehradun	82.1	94.1	88.4	25.9	77.0	52.9

Source: DLHS- RCH Round-2, 2002.

Health

Health is a key aspect of development, and available health facilities, both preventive and curative are also a crucial determinant of the quality of life that people enjoy. This is also an area in which public initiative is extremely important. The Health Policy in India emphasizes mother and child health through various methods. The lowering of infant mortality rate goes hand in hand with population control, and hence infant and child mortality are two indicators of health that are of great significance. Graph 3 compares the rural urban disparity in infant mortality and crude death rate in Uttarakhand, with that of India. Urban infant mortality rate in the state is lower than the all India level but that in the rural sector is nearly as high as the national rate. Crude death rate in the state in the rural sector is even higher than the national rate. This underlines the rural urban disparity in health conditions.

Graph 3
Vital Rates in Uttarakhand and India

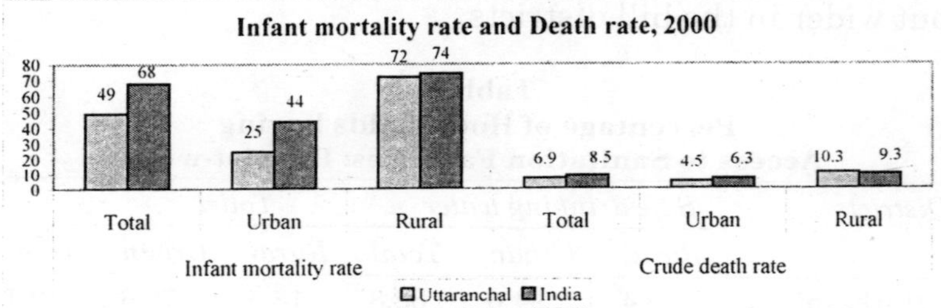

Available data on child immunisation, a significant preventive health care mechanism, demonstrates the privileged position of the urban sector (Table 9). Remarkably, in Almora and Pithoragarh, 100% of the children up to 1 year age are immunised. Only in Nainital, the rural people are found leading. Haridwar, U.S. Nagar and Dehradun have very poor performance in both sectors.

Table 9
Complete (infants) Immunization Status

District	*Total*	*Rural*	*Urban*
Uttarkashi	50.2	49.2	70.0
Almora	79.4	78.5	100.0
Tehri Garhwal	66.5	66.0	76.9
Pithorgarh	79.2	77.2	100.0
Garhwal	78.5	77.1	90.4
Chamoli	78.0	77.0	83.3
Hardwar	48.2	43.3	64.7
Udham Singh Nagar	66.7	66.1	68.6
Nainital	82.6	85.0	77.9
Dehradun	64.9	60.5	70.2

Source: DLHS-RCH 1998-99.

Efforts to promote child survival are a very important policy objective. Analysis of NFHS-2 data (Workshop Proceeding, Reproductive child health and population policy issues in Uttarakhand, 2002) showed that antenatal care of pregnant women is one way of doing this. Mothers of only 44% of children received such checkups, which is lower than the all India average. The percentage of checkups was more than double in the urban areas (78%) compared to rural areas (35%). Neonatal death is often prevented by tetanus injections administered during pregnancy. More than half of the mothers in the state received two or more doses, but it was less in rural areas (49%) than in urban areas (77%). The coverage varied with the birth order and education of the mother.

Graph 4
Place of Delivery-Home

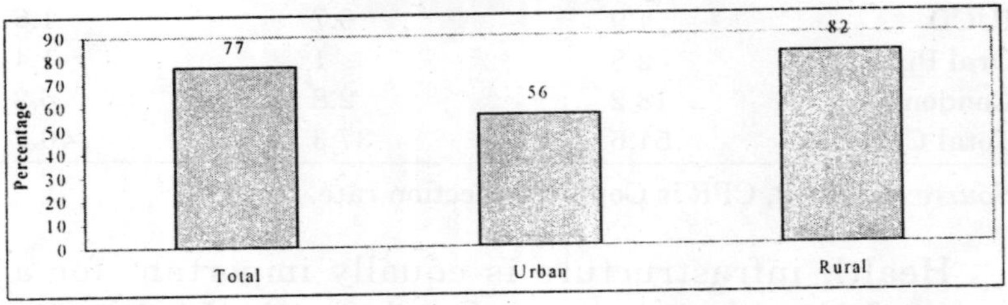

Source: NFHS-2.

Institutional delivery in hygienic conditions and trained supervision also improves survival. But Uttarakhand has only a small share of child deliveries under institutional care with majority of the birth taking place at home (Graph 4). About 82% rural households and 56% urban households still have deliveries at home. The institutional delivery was also associated with the order of birth and education of mother and also goes with higher chances of follow-up check-up. Traditional birth attendants supervise 46% of births. Immunization against common childhood diseases has been an integral component of mother and health services in India since adoption of the primary health care approach in 1978, reinforced by the declaration of the Health Policy in 1983. Family welfare also includes efficient birth control methods, which help in population stabilisation. In the state, less than 41% of the couples are protected. Among these, more than half the couples in the urban areas are using one of the contraception methods, while the rate is only 37.3% in rural areas. The rate of sterilisation is higher for rural people while the rate of condom based method is only 2.8 (Table 10).

Table 10
Modern Contraceptive Prevalence (%) among Currently Married Women (15 to 49 Years)

Methods	*Urban*	*Rural*	*Total*
Sterilization	25.7	32.8	31.1
IUCD	4.9	0.7	1.6
Oral Pill	2.8	1	1.4
Condoms	18.2	2.8	6.2
Total CPR	51.6	37.3	40.7

Source: NFHS-2, CPR is Couple protection rate.

Health infrastructure is equally important for a successful health programme. Rural areas in the state are served by a network of rural primary, block level and additional health centres, allopathic dispensaries and district hospitals. While facilities within close proximity is important, urban health infrastructure also has an important role for providing specialised, large scale and trained facilities for medical care for rural as well as urban people. Hence in this case, disparities cannot be measured in the usual way due to the complementarities between the two systems. Table 11 provides the facilities in rural and urban sectors as of 2002. While the differences do not speak much, what remains to be said is that facilities are far from adequate and inadequacy in the urban sector makes things worse for the rural people.

Table 11

Health Infrastructure in Rural and Urban Uttarakhand

Rural	*CHC*	*BPHC*	*APHC*	*SAD*	*SC*	*MC*	*RFH*	*CH*
Rudraprayag	1	3	6	23	62	3	2	0
Bageshwar	1	3	6	13	59	3	1	0
Uttarkashi	1	4	8	22	66	4	3	0
Almora	3	11	21	40	181	11	2	2
Tehri Garhwal		9	16	32	128	9	5	1
Pithorgarh	1	8	13	32	145	8	4	0
Pauri Garhwal	2	15	16	67	203	15	10	3
Chamoli	2	7	7	23	91	7	3	0
Champawat	1	3	4	10	45	3	1	0
Hardwar	3	5	19	2	139	5		1
Udham Singh Nagar	4	4	28	8	152	4	2	1
Nainital	1	8	11	32	127	8	2	4
Dehradun	3	4	18	25	129	4	3	3
Total	23	84	173	329	1527	84	38	15

Urban	*PPC district*	*PPC tehsil*	*FW Centre*	*ESI Dispensary*	*GOI Hospital*	*Voluntary Hospital*
Rudraprayag	–	–	–	–	–	2
Bageshwar	–	–	–	–	–	–
Uttarkashi	1.00	1.00	1.00	–	–	1
Almora	1.00	1.00	1.00	–	–	3
Tehri Garhwal	1.00	1.00	–	–	–	–
Pithorgarh	1.00	–	1	–	–	2
Pauri Garhwal	1.00	2.00	1.00	–	1.00	5
Chamoli	1.00	1.00	1.00	–	–	–
Champawat	–	2.00	–	–	–	2
Hardwar	1.00	1.00	–	–	6	5
Udham Singh Nagar	1.00	1.00	–	1.00	–	2
Nainital	1.00	2.00	–	–	2	3
Dehradun	1.00	2.00	2.00	3.00	8.00	4.00
Total	10.00	14.00	7.00	4.00	17.00	29.00

CHC = Community Health Centre; BPHC = Block Community Health Centre; APHC = Additional Primary Health Centre; SAD = State Allopathic Dispensary; SC = Sub Centre; MC = Main Centre PPC = Pospartum Centre; ESI = Employees State Insurance; GOI = Government of India RFH = Rural Female Hospital, CH = Combined Hospital

Source: DLHS-RCH Round-2, 2002.

Education and Human Resource Utilisation

It is now increasingly being recognized that education is a 'capability' (Sen, 1999, 2003) and that 'investment in man' may be considered even more important than physical and tangible capital formation (Myrdal, 1957, 1968). The sources of modern economic growth may be found more in changing quality of labour and capital than in accumulation of conventional units of physical capital and increased application of hours of labour (Kuznets, 1966). The decade of the 1990s is noted for some landmark initiatives with regard to the economy and society in India and not least among them is the goal of extending primary, elementary and other school education to the common people, especially in the vast and lagging rural regions. The National Education Policy and the UNDP's inclusion of education as a component of human development provided an impetus to the spread of education, especially school education in India. While education has several social and inter-generational benefits, no less significant is the visible impact it can make of the economic standards of the people and to the human resource utilisation of the country. This is possible provided opportunities exist and the quality of education is consistent with the demands of the market.

Literacy is a minimum measure of educational attainments of a society. Although Uttarakhand enjoys a higher literacy relative to many other states and all India average, the rural urban difference is wide, as seen in Graph 5. The gap is evident for both male and female populations. NFHS findings (Table 12) show that nearly 32% of urban females and 64% of rural females have not even attained primary education and a similar gap exists for those with incomplete primary education. On the other hand, 32% of the females and 37% of the males in urban areas have gained at least higher secondary education as compared to the corresponding proportions of 4.8% and 12% respectively in the rural areas.

Graph 5
Literacy in Uttarakhand, 2001

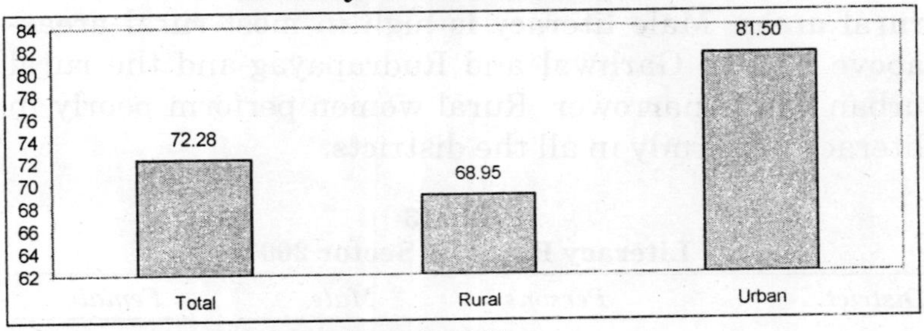

Source: Census of Uttarakhand, 2001.

Table 12
Percentage Distribution of the Household Population by Education Level

Background characteristics	*Urban*	*Rural*	*Total*
Female Education			
Illiterate	18.8	44.8	38.9
Literate, incomplete primary school	13.1	19	17.7
Primary school complete	14.9	16.6	16.2
Middle school complete	11.1	9	9.4
High school complete	10.1	5.9	6.8
Higher secondary complete and above	32	4.8	10.9
All female above age 6+	588	2,023	2,611
Male Education			
Illiterate	9.6	13.5	12.6
Literate, incomplete primary school	19.5	23.1	22.3
Primary school complete	11.4	21.3	19
Middle school complete	8.9	16.9	15
High school complete	13.4	12.9	13
Higher secondary complete and above	37.4	12.1	18
All female above age 6+	573	1,878	2,451

Source: NFHS-2, 1998-99.

The rural urban disparity in literacy is uniformly wide in all districts (Table 13). Literacy rate in the urban sector is above 80% but that in the rural area falls short of 70%

in most cases. The sectoral difference is wider for females (nearly 20% difference) than for males. The former exceeds 20% in 9 of the 13 districts and is highest in Uttarkashi, Teri Garhwal and Hardwar. The gender gap is wide in rural areas. Male literacy is high in most rural areas-above 90% in Garhwal and Rudrapayag-and the rural urban gap is narrower. Rural women perform poorly in literacy uniformly in all the districts.

Table 13
Literacy Rates by Sector 2001

District	*Persons*		*Male*		*Female*	
	Rural	*Urban*	*Rural*	*Urban*	*Rural*	*Urban*
Uttarakhand	68.95	81.50	82.74	87.21	55.52	74.77
Rudraprayag	74.14	81.67	90.90	82.14	59.84	80.51
Bageshwar	71.44	86.86	88.47	90.78	56.77	81.98
Uttarkashi	64.70	87.46	83.55	93.93	45.10	78.48
Almora	72.73	92.54	89.47	95.47	59.31	88.68
Tehri Garhwal	64.82	86.67	84.84	90.78	47.34	79.91
Pithorgarh	74.51	90.19	89.81	95.34	60.40	84.33
Garhwal	76.41	88.28	91.25	92.66	64.01	82.94
Chamoli	74.17	88.95	89.08	93.96	60.54	81.98
Champawat	69.44	80.51	88.32	87.20	51.93	72.69
Hardwar	58.16	77.91	70.56	84.14	44.15	70.52
Udham Singh	62.88	71.56	74.54	79.48	50.11	62.50
Nainital	78.02	82.40	87.62	87.00	67.61	77.16
Dehradun	71.42	85.35	80.42	90.37	61.57	79.61

Source: Census of India 2001, Series-6.

Haridwar and US Nagar fall short in rural male literacy although the rural urban gap for males at the state level is moderate (83% versus 87%). However, female literacy is 55.5% for rural Uttarakhand compared to 75% in urban areas. It is particularly low in Uttarkashi (45%), Tehri Garhwal (47%) and Champawat (52%), all of which has more than 80% male literacy in the sector. US Nagar and Haridwar are the districts where male and female literacy are both low. The gender gap is narrower in urban areas. Female literacy is highly skewed with higher than average rates in most districts. Thus, although Uttarakhand is a good performer in terms of overall literacy rate, there is immense rural urban disparity, and gender gap-especially in rural areas. There are pockets of illiteracy scattered all over the state but Haridwar and Udham Singh Nagar perform particularly badly and require policy attention (Graph 6).

Graph 6
Rural Literacy Rates in Uttarakhand Districts

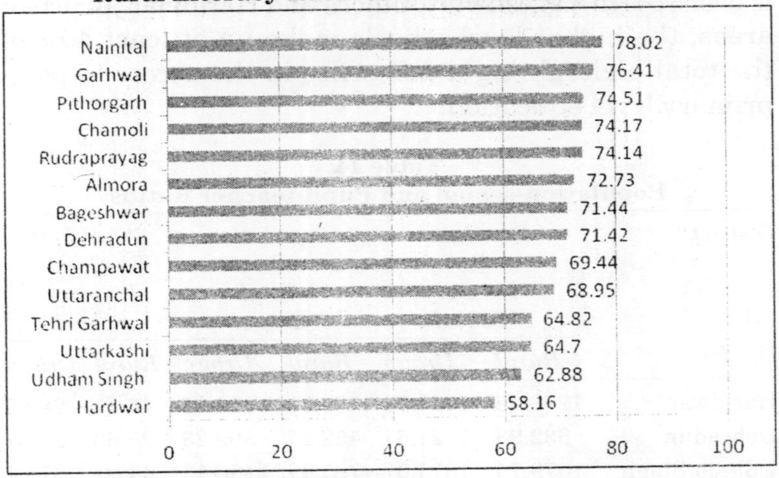

Source: Census of Uttarakhand, 2001.

While literacy and educational attainments are outcomes of initiatives taken in the past, the seeds of future development can be found in the attempts at social infrastructure development in the present. The decade of the nineties saw the creation of educational network with a focus on rural and remote areas and on marginalized sections. Establishment of school infrastructure is an essential starting point of such an endevour. In Uttarakhand, a primary school is provided for every 375 people living in the rural areas and the total number of schools is far larger than that in urban areas.

The population coverage is larger in Haridwar (1009) but is less than the state level coverage for some hilly and rural districts. This reflects the population concentration in the urbanised districts than in the hilly ones where the population is less and also substantially dispersed. In urban areas, the population coverage is much more (Table 14), possibly as an out come of high population density. In rural areas more than 74% of all schools are primary schools (Table 16), but this share is over 78% in Bageshwar, Almora and Haridwar. In urban areas, the higher level schools make up at least 40% of the total highlighting a difference in the access to post-primary level education.

Table 14
Population-school and Pupil-teacher Ratios

District	*Population Per Primary School*		*Population Per Total School*		*Pupil Per Teacher in Primary School*	
	Rural	*Urban*	*Rural*	*Urban*	*Rural*	*Urban*
Haridwar	1293.46	1720.71	1009.66	1114.16	46.71	28.80
Dehradun	632.98	1521.61	452.27	899.23	25.66	22.36
Udham Singh Nagar	1079.75	1875.07	785.09	1155.13	44.88	37.77
Nainital	520.18	1605.87	371.05	973.96	25.82	29.15
Garhwal	351.26	1388.03	251.09	745.64	22.46	21.99
Almora	406.27	1147.85	317.98	674.36	25.91	17.26
Tehri Garhwal	386.78	1044.20	280.07	602.84	26.04	21.32
Pithorgarh	353.99	1122.48	272.68	652.60	21.57	19.59
Chamoli	337.86	740.07	251.47	467.78	23.06	15.66
Uttarkashi	362.16	849.04	267.25	498.35	23.63	19.06
Bageshwar	408.88	867.00	322.63	650.25	26.62	27.26
Rudraprayag	402.76	388.71	285.93	226.75	24.78	19.03
Champawat	402.79	1558.76	305.78	884.70	30.34	26.95
Uttarakhand	506.12	1511.31	375.02	913.40	28.49	26.38

Source: NCERT, 2000.

A substantial share of the school buildings are however, not *pucca* structures, especially in rural areas. In the rural areas in only seven out of the thirteen districts, more than 70% schools have *pucca* structures. The same shares are high in urban areas varying from 79% in Champawat to 96% in Bageshwar (Table 16a) Enrolments in rural schools are larger in more populated districts for both boys and girls. The urban sector in hilly Champawat also has a relatively high enrolment rate (Table 15). The pupil to teacher ratio is marginally higher in the rural sector and varies directly with population. Higher schools are less in number than primary schools. In the rural sector, the number of these higher schools is about a quarter of the number of primary schools. However, the situation is much better in the urban sector.

Table 15
Enrolment in Classes I-V

District	*Rural*			*Urban*		
	Boys	*Girls*	*Total*	*Boys*	*Girls*	*Total*
Haridwar	75785	63143	138928	29444	24416	53860
Dehradun	41209	38779	79988	40347	34247	74594
US Nagar	62471	54270	116741	28534	23778	52312
Nainital	32857	31792	64649	16830	14716	31546
Garhwal	39157	40059	79216	5312	4489	9801
Almora	39216	42358	81574	4122	3297	7419
Tehri Garhwal	44398	45270	89668	4698	3819	8517
Pithorgarh	26840	28804	55644	3828	3266	7094
Chamoli	23370	24213	47583	3473	2806	6279
Uttarkashi	21769	21975	43744	1526	1217	2743
Bageshwar	15870	17232	33102	842	603	1445
Rudraprayag	16453	17009	33462	435	351	786
Champawat	14783	15502	30285	2629	2108	4737
Uttarakhand	439395	424904	864299	142020	119113	261133

Note: Districts are arranged by total Population.
Source: NCERT, 2000.

Table 16a
Primary and Higher Schools in Districts

District	*Rural*			*Urban*		
	Primary School	*Others School*	*Total School*	*Primary School*	*Others School*	*Total School*
Haridwar	772	217	989	259	141	400
Dehradun	951	380	1331	445	308	753
Udham Singh Nagar	770	289	1059	215	134	349
Nainital	948	381	1329	168	109	277
Garhwal	1727	689	2416	65	56	121
Almora	1419	394	1813	47	33	80
Tehri Garhwal	1412	538	1950	56	41	97
Pithorgarh	1147	342	1489	50	36	86
Chamoli	946	325	1271	67	39	106
Uttarkashi	749	266	1015	27	19	46
Bageshwar	591	158	749	9	3	12
Rudraprayag	558	228	786	7	5	12
Champawat	476	151	627	21	16	37
Uttarakhand	12466	4358	16824	1436	940	2376

Note: Others School include Upper Primary, Secondary and Higher Secondary School. Districts are arranged by total population.

Education has the important role of creating human capital and this should in turn be reflected in the employment pattern and income generating capacity of the people. With respect to employment, it is well known that the rural and urban sectors differ in terms of the nature of the occupations pursued. Graph 7 shows a highly non-diversified distribution of occupational pattern. Agriculture occupies nearly 72% of the rural workers including about 62% who are actually cultivators and less than 10% working as agricultural labour. In the urban areas agriculture and household industries occupy a little more than 8% of the workers. The concentration is most evident for rural women of whom, about 82.3% are cultivators and 6.2% are agricultural labours. Despite the high work participation rates seen in Chapter 2. This concentration in agriculture reflects the lack of job opportunities of women outside agriculture (see Chapter two, Table 6).

Graph 7
Occupation Patterns by Sectors

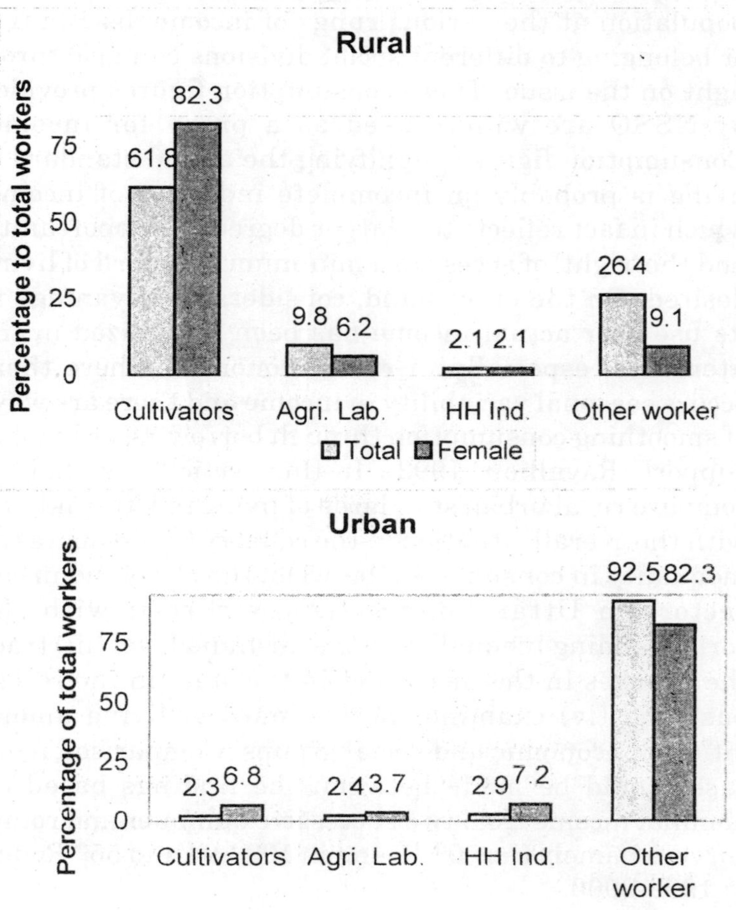

Source: State Planning Department, Govt. of Uttarakhand.

ECONOMIC DISPARITY

It is possible to throw light on the economic disparity between rural and urban regions within Indian states by analysing the consumer expenditures data for the two sectors reported by the NSSO in its quinquinnial surveys. Comparison of the consumption of sections of the population at the various rungs of income distribution or belonging to different social divisions can also throw light on the issue. These consumption figures provided by NSSO are widely used as a proxy for income. Consumption figures, signifying the actual standard of living is probably an incomplete indicator of income, which in fact reflects to a larger degree the 'opportunity' and the 'right' of access to a minimum standard of living desired. On the other hand, considerable advantage in its use over actual income has been recognized in the literature, especially in rural economies where there occurs seasonal variability in income and there are ways of smoothing consumption through borrowing or kinship support (Ravallion, 1992). In this section, we shall (i) compare rural urban standards of living in Uttarakhand with the overall situation in the country (ii) estimate the inequality in consumption between the rural and urban sectors in Uttarakhand and compare it with the corresponding inequality at the all-India level (iii) trace the changes in the inequality in the state in the recent past and (iv) examine the standard of living among different economic and social groups. Comparison in all cases could be made between the findings based on nominal income from two successive quinquennial round surveys namely the 50th Round in 1993-94 and 55th Round in 1999-2000.

Use of Consumption Expenditure data

There arise however two serious problems in using the consumption expenditure data. The first problem is that in the literature on poverty, an active debate has been going on about the comparability of the findings from 55th Round with the earlier ones. The calculation of the poverty rates are done on the basis of the NSSO surveys. The reference period used by NSSO in its quinquennial round surveys 1972-3 (27 Round), 1977-78 (32 Round) 1983 (38 Round) 1987-88 (43 Round) and 1993-94 (50 Round) was last month or 'last 30 days' for all items of budget. However, in order to eliminate effects of seasonal and other transitory factors, a period of 'last 365 days' was included in addition to 'last 30 days' for some item groups from Round 32 onwards. The choice of the reference period (one month) was based on the experience gained in the early NSS rounds, especially the 4th and 5th rounds and some field tests carried out by Mahalanobis and Sen (1954). Later on, doubts were expressed on the suitability of the period used by NSSO as shorter recall period was used for shorter frequency items elsewhere in the world. The disagreement between NSSO based and National Accounts (CSO) based estimates of private expenditure further called for a review of the procedures. As an initial step, comparative studies were carried out, involving recall periods 'last week' and 'last month' assigned randomly to different households in annual (thin sample) enquiries during 51st-54th Rounds for food pan tobacco and intoxicants and elicited a considerable divergence in reporting. In NSS quinquennial 55th Round however, two different periods i.e., 7 days and 30 days were used in a single schedule. The difference in the reported consumption for the two periods was significantly lower, reflecting a reconciling act. The 30-day question in 55th Round elicited higher consumption figures, which were enough to drastically reduce poverty rates. While the multiple reporting period incorporated in the 55th Round and the shorter recall period for high frequency items have been considered desirable (Ravallion, 1992) and with 'the potential to produce excellent results' (Deaton, 2001), Sen and Himanshu (2004) challenged the comparability of such data on expenditure and poverty, describing the retention of the 30 days food question as a 'last minute compromise'. This change in the methodology pertaining to recall periods in consumer surveys have made comparison of incomes between the period unreliable. The problem is as yet unresolved but the comparability per se is ruled out in academic discussions. This paper presents the corresponding findings from the 50th and the 55th Rounds but any comparison is totally avoided here. However, comparisons between inequality measures have been attempted based on the rationale that information on expenditure reported with a given recall period are possibly subject to the same bias if any in both sectors. Thus under any hypothetical presumption of over-reporting in the case of 55th Round survey, it is assumed that households in both sectors are equally likely to over-report. Inequality measured by an acceptable measure then remains unbiased. The inequality measures employed as coefficients, ratios or indices are scale neutral with respect to income.

Any analysis of the lower income groups of the population defined by a conventionally fixed 'poverty line' also becomes difficult in light of the methodological changes. The poverty line in India evolved with the estimation by a Working group in the 1960s based on the recommendations of the ICMR and by various economists including Dandekar and Rath seventies and the redefinition by 'The Task force on projection of Minimum Needs and Effective consumption Demand' in the late 1970s. With an intake of 2400 calories in rural areas and 2100 calories in urban areas accepted as nutritional norms, the poverty line is regularly updated in terms of the purchasing power needed to meet this specific calorie intake standard with some margin for nonfood consumption needs. In fact in the 55th round, the poverty figures have come down drastically even at the all India level, an outcome that has been associated with the change in methodology rather than the paradigm. Identification of the lower income segments through relative poverty seems conceptually acceptable and is also widely used in literature on inequality[1]. Thus, to avoid confusion, the lower 25% percentile of households of Uttarakhand in each round has been selected to study their social composition and comparison over time. The poor referred to in this section of the study therefore may not cover all households deemed as 'poor' by the absolute and conventional poverty line but are definitely in the lowest level of economic hierarchy. For assessing the intensity of poverty in a recent period, the distribution or occurrence of lower MPCE classes (defined by all India lowest deciles) are examined in the light of similar distribution elsewhere.

The second problem in using this data is that, Uttarakhand is a recently carved out state, and the relevant information is subsumed in the overall information on Uttar Pradesh of which it was a part. To uncover the information on the specific regions, we therefore had to analyse the unit or household level data obtained in NSSO database and identify the state using relevant codes for regions and districts as available and suggested by NSSO.

Standards of Living and Disparity

We analyse disparity in this section in terms of the monthly per capita consumption expenditure (MPCE) figures with a 30 days recall. Table 16a and 16b give a comparative view of Uttarakhand in terms of average levels of living (MPCE) and the prevalence of low standards of living. The people with low standards of living are those with MPCE in the lowest all-India MPCE classes. Rural-urban disparity is assessed with the help of the (i) gap (Urban-Rural), and (ii) ratio (Urban/Rural).

Table 16b
Uttarakhand MPCE in Comparative View (Rs)

	50th ROUND		*55th ROUND*	
	Rural	*Urban*	*Rural*	*Urban*
Region				
Uttarakhand	299	518	551	836
Utter Pradesh	274	389	466	690
India	281	458	486	855
Consumer Price Index (CPI)	520	618	833	998

Note: Base for CPI 1972-73.

Table 16b shows that as far as MPCE is concerned, Uttarakhand had a better position than the parent state of Uttar Pradesh and the national average even in the initial parts of the nineties. This applied for both the rural and the urban sectors. Urban MPCE in the 55th Round is lower than the all India level, although it is substantially higher than Uttar Pradesh. The rural MPCE at Rs. 551 is much higher than the national average MPCE of Rs. 486. The rural urban disparity measured as a gap or the absolute difference in nominal MPCEs, was higher for Uttarakhand than for Uttar Pradesh or India in the 50th Round result. However, it is less than that for India, though somewhat higher than Uttar Pradesh, in the 55th Round. The increase in the rural urban nominal gap in MPCE is only 30% for the state compared to 95% and 108% for Uttar Pradesh and India and the rise in consumer price index at the all India level of around 60% in both sectors.

The people with low standards living (less than Rs. 225 per month) constitute only 0.6% of rural Uttarakhand. The neighbouring states mostly have an even better record except in the case of Uttar Pradesh, where the share is nearly 4%. The situation is similar for the other higher classes. In the urban sector the shares are higher and are similarly higher than in most other states, although by a smaller margin. The urban poverty situation is relatively worse, in a way reflecting the rural situation from where people migrate for a livelihood to the urban areas.

Table 17
Distribution of Population in Uttarakhand and Neighbouring States in All India Lowest MPCE Classes-55th Round

State	*Rural*				*Urban*			
MPCE less than Rs.	225	255	300	340	300	350	425	500
Uttarakhand	0.6	3.1	8.9	16.5	4.0	8.4	14.1	19.3
Himachal	0.2	0.5	2.5	4.3	0	2.2	4.8	7.3
Haryana	0.7	1.2	2.7	5.7	3.0	4.0	10.4	16.1
Uttar Pradesh	4.4	9.5	20.8	32.1	10.1	18.7	32.5	44.3
Punjab	0.1	0.6	1.8	4.0	0.9	2.9	8.6	19.4

Note: All India lowest classes 5%, 10%, 20%, 30% are respectively MPCE < Rs 225, MPCE < Rs 255, MPCE < Rs 300 & MPCE < Rs 340 for Rural sector and MPCE < Rs 300, MPCE < Rs 350, MPCE < Rs 425 & MPCE < Rs 500 respectively for Urban sector.

Source: Sarvekshana, 2001 and Authors' calculations.

As is the case all over India, the agricultural labour mostly feels the incidence of the low level of income, followed by other labour while the self-employed in agriculture are better off. In the urban areas, again similar to the national scenario, casual labour make up the highest proportion of this section of the population while regular salaried workers are the lowest (Table 18).

To find out if rural-urban disparity levels in consumption apply to all sections of populations we have considered select MPCE classes and social groups. Table 18 shows the MPCE levels of different dominant religious groups suggesting that the Sikh community has moved to the highest position in rural Uttarakhand while in the urban sector it has retained its pre-eminence. In all the social cases the urban population has a higher MPCE than its rural counter part. MPCE has increased in absolute terms but the urban-rural ratio has fallen in all cases except for the Sikh community, for whom the ratio has remained almost the same as before.

Table 18
Percentage of Population in All India Lowest Two Deciles by Household Type-55th Round

	Rural			*Urban*	
Employment type	*Uttara-khand*	*India*	*Employ-ment type*	*Uttara-khand*	*India*
1R	10.5	16.8	1U	17.1	22.2
2R	21.6	32.9	2U	8.0	9.3
3R	14.7	20.0	3U	31.3	44.4
4R	6.6	13.8	4U	17.2	13.7
5R	8.1	11.0			

Note: 1R = self employed in non-agriculture, 2R = Agricultural labour, 3R = Other labour, 4R = Self employed in agriculture 5R = Others, 1 U = Self employed, 2U = Regular wage/salary earning, 3U = Casual labour, 4U = Others. Lowest two deciles are Rs. 300 in rural and Rs. 425 in urban sectors.

Source: NSSO.

In figure 8 the disparity in 1999-2000 appears more severe relative to Uttar Pradesh, where both rural and urban MPCEs are lower relatively to Uttarakhand, but is less than the all India level. Considering the MPCE classes in Table 4.20, the sectoral disparity is seen to exist in all cases i.e., among the poorest and the richest quantiles, but the degree of disparity appears to have declined over time. Thus the top 10% and 25% urban population is 1.71 and 1.47 times richer than the corresponding rural population, while the same proportions were higher at 1.85 and 1.92 in the 50th Round. In the same way, the poorer 10% and 25% population in the rural sector have come closer to urban sector with time. This is particularly because of the significant improvement of the ratio

Graph 8
Rural Urban Disparity in Comparison (MPCE)

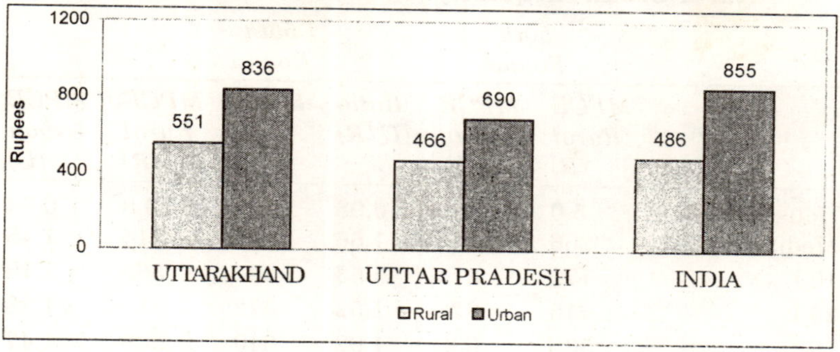

corresponding to the lowest decile where the urban to rural ratio has come down from 1.53 to 1.19. The narrowing is reflected in the median income also. Such comparisons of MPCE show that Uttarakhand, which has relatively better position with respect to rural sector even at the start of the 1990s has a narrower rural urban gap relative to India. The development process and the government's proactive actions may have treated the rural sector more favourably than the urban sector (Graph 8). However the rural urban disparity still exists both in overall terms and in various sections of the population (Table 19).

Table 19
Average MPCE Across Dominant Social and Religious Groups (Rs)

	Muslims	*Hindus*	*Sikhs*	*Scheduled Caste*	*Scheduled Tribe*
050th Round					
Rural	342	301	298	293	285
Urban	451	501	805	424	559
Ratio (U/R)	1.32	1.67	2.70	1.45	1.96
55th Round					
Rural	516	552	717	477	498
Urban	533	824	1924	621	768
Ratio (U/R)	1.03	1.49	2.68	1.30	1.54

Source: Authors' calculations.

Table 20
Rural Urban Inequality Across Deciles As Ratios

	50th Round			*55th Round*		
	MPCE Rural (R)	*MPCE Urban (U)*	*Ratio (U/R)*	*Rural (R)*	*MPCE Rural (R)*	*MPCE Urban (U)*
Household Size	5.0	4.9	0.98	6.2	5.8	0.94
Median	266	441	1.66	491	714	1.45
10 L	179	274	1.53	304	363	1.19
25 L	215	328	1.52	372	514	1.38
75 L	332	638	1.92	640	939	1.47
90 L	459	848	1.85	830	1416	1.71

Note: MPCE are percentile figures starting from lowest.
Source: Authors' calculations.

An Index of Inequality

A composite measure of inequality is useful for summarising the rural urban disparity in income. Any inequality index as a measure of welfare is considered desirable if it satisfies properties like mean independence and Pigou-Dalton principle of transfer[2] and a number of such indices are used in the literature with varying merits and limitations. Another important property of indices that can be useful in this study is additive decomposability (Shorrocks, 2004). An index is additively decomposable if it can be neatly expressed as the sum of a 'between group' and a 'within group' term when the population is broken up into a number of exhaustive groups. Conceptually, the 'between group' component is defined as the value of inequality index when all the within group inequalities are assumed non-existent by a hypothetical assignment of the group average income to each member of the same group. Similarly, the within group component is defined as the value of index when all between group inequalities are suppressed by a hypothetical equalisation of group mean incomes to the overall mean by an equiproportionate change in the income within each group. The two measures Theil's L and Theil's T are found to possess the decomposable properties[3]. Further, the Theil measure L is said to be 'strictly' decomposable and preferable since the elimination of between group inequality does not affect the value of the within group component and reduces total inequality exactly by the same amount. Another measure of inequality, the simple coefficient of variation is unsuitable for the restrictive demands on the welfare function and above all for being mean dependent (See Sen, 1974). The coefficient of variation based on mean income can be described as the simplest measure of dispersion and being scale neutral only overcomes the latter drawback. A lognormal distribution is usually a more appropriate description of income and the variance based on the log of income (LVAR) is often deemed preferable and reported in literature. But it can lead to a perverse[4] result that makes it unsuitable although the problem is low in most empirical distributions. The most widely used measure is the Gini coefficient or the Lorenz ratio which yields a simple interpretation without asking for restrictions on the welfare function. However, a problem arises in comparing distribution when the Lorenz curves cross each other.

The choice of a usable inequality index presents a complex issue. Usually the desirable properties enumerated by Shorrocks (2004) are (i) symmetry (ii) the Pigou-Dalton principle of transfer (iii) scale invariance (iv) replication invariance and (v) zero normalisation. The Entropy family of indices satisfies all these properties. One property that will be required in the present context of measuring the rural urban disparity is decomposability into within groups and between group's components. The entropy indices T and L satisfy this condition and are useful for studying group related inequalities as in this study. In addition, the variance of the logarithm of income (N) too satisfies the desirable and the decomposability conditions and is quite widely used. But the decomposition in case of T is said to be weak as it uses group expenditure shares as weights in the within groups component whereas the other two use population shares that are unaffected when between groups inequality in eliminated.

The decomposition of inequality according to a partition of the aggregate population into geographical regions (or, more generally, into any set of mutually exclusive and exhaustive subgroups) is most often undertaken with one of the entropy indices popularised by Theil (1967, 1972) and later explored in more detail by others including, Shorrocks. The T and L indices in the entropy family may be written as

$$T = E_1(Y) = \left\{\sum_{i \in N} (y_i / \mu)(\ln y_i / \mu)\right\} /n$$

and

$$L = E_0(Y) = \frac{1}{n} \sum_{i \in N} In \frac{\mu}{y_i}$$

The decomposition properties of this class of measures are best illustrated by considering the index L and by supposing that the set of individuals, N, is partitioned into m proper subgroups N_k (k = 1,2...m), with respective income vectors Y^k, mean incomes $\bar{\mu}_k$ population sizes n_k, and population shares $v_k = n_k/n$. It will also be convenient to let yk denote the distribution obtained by replacing each income in the vector y^k with the subgroup mean μ_k. Then

$$L = E_0(y^1, y^2 \ldots Y^m) = \frac{1}{n} \sum_{k=1}^{m} \sum_{i \in n_k} In \frac{\mu}{y_i}$$

$$= \sum_{k=1}^{m} n_k / n \left(\sum_{i \in nk} \ln(\mu_k / y_i)\right) + 1/n \sum_{k=}^{m} \sum_{i \in nk} \ln(\mu / \mu_k)$$

$$= \sum_{k=1}^{m} V_k E_o(y^k) + \sum_{k=1}^{m} V_k \ln(\mu / \mu_k) = \text{W+B}$$

Where

$$\text{W} = \sum_{k=1}^{m} V_k E_o(y^k)$$

is a weighted average of subgroup inequality values, traditionally referred to as the 'within group' component of inequality; and

$$\text{B} = \sum_{k=1}^{m} V_k \ 1\text{n}(\mu / \mu) \ (\bar{y}^1, \bar{y}^2, \bar{y}^3, \ldots \bar{y}^m)$$

Where B is the 'between-group' contribution to inequality, and represents the level of inequality obtained by replacing the income of each person with the mean income of his or her respective subgroup. Thus the overall level of inequality for a region can be expressed in an intuitively appealing fashion as an exact sum of the average inequality within sub-regions and the inequality due purely to differences in average incomes between sub-regions.

We have presented simple coefficients of variation at actual values (CV) and logarithmic values (LCV) of MPCE and the Theil measures at the sectoral and aggregate levels (Table 21). The Theil index L is then further used to decompose the inequality into it's 'within' and 'between' components. Preferred for it 'strict' additive property, the overall level of inequality in the state is expressed in an intuitive fashion as an exact sum of the average inequality within the rural and urban sectors and the inequality due purely to difference in average MPCEs between the two sectors.

Comparability of results with alternatives indices is first examined. Taking first the Coefficient of Variation (CV), the dispersion seems to have increased over time. Looking at the sectoral figures, the urban sector is found to have become more unequal while inequality in rural Uttarakhand came down marginally from 0.58 to 0.56. The LVAR index however indicates a fall in inequality at all levels. Considering the two Theil measures, both indicate the same tendency–increase in urban inequality and decline in rural inequality but in contrast to the indication based on the CV, the aggregate inequality has also come down with these measures. Thus the Theil indices suggest an improvement in income distribution in the 1990s following the same trend within the rural sector.

Table 21
Income Inequality Change With Alternative Measures

NSS Rounds	*50th Round*				*55th Round*			
	CV	*LVAR*	*TH1*	*TH2*	*CV*	*LVAR*	*TH1*	*TH2*
Rural	0.581	0.235	0.098	0.116	0.563	.164	0.093	0.108
Urban	0.518	0.343	0.124	0.122	0.614	.273	0.144	0.152
Total	0.617	0.296	0.125	0.142	0.625	.211	0.121	0.139

Notes: CV = Coefficient of variation, LVAR = variance of log, TH1 = Theil l index, TH2 = Theil T index.
Source: Authors' calculations.

As outlined previously, we have used the Theil index L to decompose the inequality, in an attempt to measure the 'within' and 'between' disparity for the two sectors in Table 22. The between group inequality has fallen from 0.022 to 0.016 while the total within group inequality has gone up. The results show that, in fact, the rural-urban component of inequality has come down from 18% to 13% of total inequality.

In Uttarakhand, the inequality within the rural region is less than that within the urban region (Table 23) and this is similar to the situation at the national level in 1999-2000. The rural urban inequality for the state in 1999-2000 is 13.3% of total inequality, much less compared to the all-India figure of 19.8%. It has also shown a declining trend from compared to that (17.6 %) in 1993-94.

Table 22
Decomposition of Inequality

	(Theil 1 measure)			
	Within	*Within*	*Between*	*Within*
NSS Rounds	Rural	Urban	Group	Group
50th Round	0.098	0.125	0.022	0.103
			(17.6)	(82.4)
55th Round	0.093	0.144	0.016	0.104
			(13.3)	(86.7)

Note: Figures in parentheses are % shares.
Source: Authors' calculations.

Table 23
Inequality in comparison with all India

	Years	*Within Rural*	*Within Urban*	*Between sectors (in %)*
Uttarakhand	1993-94	.098	.125	17.6
	1999-00	.093	.144	13.3
India	1999-00	.113	.198	19.8

Source: Authors' calculations.

The Lower Percentiles

In Table 24 the rural poor, constituting the lowest 25% of the state's MPCE classes, are found to be composed of the self-employed in agriculture in both NSSO Rounds though the share of this group among the poor has come down significantly. The agricultural self-employed is a dominant group in the state. The share of those self-employed in non-agriculture among the poor has gone up from a small value of 4% to 16% while agricultural labour as well as other labour improved their lots. In the urban sector a part of the self-employed section has moved out of poverty but the casual labour group as well as the regular salaried has worsened its position.

Thus while labour classes and those in employment have not joined the poor, the self- employed in rural sector (possibly in informal and unorganised sector) have constituted higher share of the poor. Agricultural progress is indicated in the lowering share of those self employed and those wage-employed in agriculture. In the urban sector, casual labour has increased its share among the poor. Industrialisation and progress of agro-processing sector certainly need attention here.

Table 24
Distribution of Poor by Household Type (%)

Rural			*Urban*		
Household Type	*50th Round*	*55th Round*	*Household Type*	*50th Round*	*55th Round*
1R	4.2	16.2	1U	42.0	38.2
2R	14.2	10.8	2U	54.2	33.5
3R	10.9	10.3	3U	3.8	14.3
4R	60.1	47.7	4U		14.0
5R	10.6	15.0			

Note: 1R = self employed in non-agriculture, 2R = Agricultural labour, 3R = Other labour, 4R = Self employed in agriculture 5R = Others
1U = Self employed, 2U = Regular wage/salary earning, 3U = Casual labour, 4U = Others.

The improvement in income distribution found in the tables above can be attributed to direct rural alleviation policy or general developmental factors arising from the state policy actions directed to raise income and productivity. A 'trickle down' effect of the national growth process witnessed in the 1990s may not be ruled out in this hilly and tourism oriented and forest based state via greater opportunities in non-agricultural enterprises through greater demand. Similar growth elsewhere has helped to bring in remittances from migrant member of households, who have obtained earning opportunity elsewhere.

Table 25
Rural Poor Households Benefited (%)

	IRDP Assistance	*Public Works*	*Pension*	*Remittance*	*Non-agricultural income*
50th round	93.1	4.9	0.1	1.8	4.2
55th round	7.9	12.9	6.9	24.0	22.0

Source: Author's calculations.

Some of the most commonly discussed schemes are IRDP loans, public works programmes and pension schemes. The improvement of positions of those employed in agriculture as self-employed and labourers indicate the effects of such policy and agrarian development. Table 4.25 however reveals that the poverty programmes benefited only a small section of the poor. The role of IRDP became weaker while public works programs and the pension scheme have become more important. The proportion of rural poor households benefited by remittances and non-agricultural income is much higher, above 20% in the 55th Round.

Notes

1. The absolute poverty line, also drawn in the light of a socially acceptable minimal standard of living, also catches an aspect of relative inequality (Sen, 1974) as the line itself will be higher in a country with relatively higher average standard of living.
2. Mean independence (or homogeneity in income of degree zero) means that the index remains unchanged if everyone's income is changed in the same proportion. The transfer principle implies that any transfer from a richer to a poorer household that does not reverse their relative ranks reduces the value of the index.
3. The Gini coefficient is not sub-group consistent, an intuitively appealing property satisfied by the Entropy family whereby an increase in inequality within a group

must not lead to a decrease in total inequality keeping the group mean incomes and population sizes fixed and the coefficient is therefore not amenable to decomposition. However this serious drawback has not discouraged many researchers from attempting decomposition of the Gini index in specific contexts (Shorrocks, 2004).

4. A transfer from a poorer person to a richer person may reduce the magnitude of the index for high-income levels.

5

SAMPLE DESIGN AND DETAILS OF PRIMARY SURVEY

The rest of the chapters in this book analyze rural urban disparity in Uttarakhand on the basis of a primary survey. This chapter describes the design of the survey and discusses the nature of the sample that is chosen for this purpose. It attempts to present some first-hand ground-level information on the issue by seeking the views and reactions of residents of Uttarakhand. This is done through interviews of individuals and soliciting responses to scheduled queries from households. The main objective of this survey is to supplement the secondary data based information on rural urban disparities and rural development issues in Uttarakhand. The analysis of the primary data in the subsequent chapters aims to capture the summary of social realities in the rural and urban areas of the state, with particular reference to employment, quality of life, health, and education.

METHODOLOGY OF SAMPLING

The primary survey covers a single cross-section of the state and the design was largely based on the requirements of this study. Three urban centers had to be chosen purposively keeping in view the (i) occupation profile of the population and ensuring (ii) geographical dispersion. Once these urban centers had been selected, the next step was to choose the villages from those situated around these urban centres. Census data and information from Village and Town directories (1981) have been used for the selection process. The Census data from 1991 giving details of the districts is used as a frame and this provided the nine districts falling in the Himalayan region of Uttar Pradesh. However as there have been some reorganisation of the districts and creation of new ones, the actual selection had to be made from the current list of districts.

Table 1
Sample Town Profile

Town	*Area Sq. Km*	*House-hold No.*	*Popu-lation*	*Manu-facturing %*	*Trade %*	*Ser-vices %*	*Main workers %*
Haldwani	10.62	18613	104195	3.96	8.23	14.95	28
Uttarkashi M.B.	12.02	3310	13919	2.36	5.37	22.44	34
Rishikesh M.B.	1.6	9335	44487	6.26	9.13	14.36	30

Source: Census 1981 (Village and Town Directory).
Note: Main workers reported for the districts.

Uttarakhand is roughly triangular in shape. The districts of Chamoli/Uttarkashi from the northeast, Dehradun/Haridwar from west and Nainital/Pithorgarh from east can be considered to be representative of the different geographical locations. As explained earlier, the Census districts are examined on the basis of census data 1991 while keeping in mind the formation of new districts that exist today. The districts are compared in terms of the share of their urban population engaged in (i) manufacturing and processing in household and other than household industries (ii) trade and commerce and (iii) services in terms of transport, storage, communication, construction and others services.

The occupational patterns considered have been broadly laid down in the purposive sampling scheme. Construction is included in the services category. From the current list of districts, Nainital, Rudraprayag and Dehradun were found to have relatively high and balanced share of manufacturing, trade and services. However, Rudraprayag is a new district mostly carved out of Chamoli in 1991, and although it was a natural choice due to the dominance of the relevant sectors, the constitution of this district involved reorganisation at the *tehsil* level of Chamoli district along with some other districts. As a result, the villages listed in 1981 and 1991 census do not match with the present status. For these reasons, Uttarkashi has been selected instead of Rudraprayag. Thus the three districts chosen were Nainital, Uttarkashi and Dehradun. Of these three districts, Uttarkashi falls in the hills completely and has a higher altitude (1158 metres) on the average. Both Dehradun and Nainital have got substantial segments in the plains also, are more urbanised by population share and the average altitudes at 356 mtrs. and 423 mtrs. are lower. Uttarkashi is the most remote district at an estimated distance of 391 km from capital Delhi and is connected only by roadways. Dehradun (236 km) and Nainital (297 km) are nearer to Delhi and have railway connectivity as well as airports. The three districts make up nearly a third of the state in area and population. About 34% of the urban population and 28% of rural population of Uttarakhand live in these districts.

The next step is the choice of the urban centres and urban households. Disaggregated census (1991) data on these three districts are (i) classified by working out the occupational shares at the level of urban centres/Towns summed over wards and (ii) chosen by the same criteria of occupational patterns used for the selection of the districts. In the choice of urban centres, the population was also considered to be an important factor and hence in Dehradun, Rishikesh was preferred over Doiwala on this consideration The three selected urban centres were (i) Rishikesh in Dehradun District (ii) Haldwani cum Kathgodam M.B. in Nainital District and (iii) Uttarkashi M.B in Uttarkashi district (Table 5.1). In order to choose the urban households, the urban population is stratified by the type of occupation of the head of household. These are (i) Government Employees (ii) Employees of organized sectors both government and private (iii) Self-employed in business and services (iv) Self employed in petty business and vendors (v) Skilled daily wage earners (vi) Unskilled daily wage earners and (vii) Others. Three Wards were selected from each center according to occupational characteristics and 40 households were selected from each ward giving a total of 120 households in each center and 360 households in the urban sector as a whole.

The final step is to choose the villages and village households. Six villages were selected around each urban center (Table 2). These were at increasing distances from the urban center (UC) but within a radius of about 30 to 40 KM that demarcates the hinterland of that urban area. The Village and Town Directory (1981) provides information on villages and their distance from the nearest urban center along with other relevant variables. The villages are grouped as (i) least remote i.e., 1 to 10 Km from the UC, (ii) remote i.e., 11 to 20 Km from the UC and (iii) most remote i.e., 31 Km or more from the UC. Usually this category ranges from 31 to 40 Km. In the case of a large district Uttarkashi-with little urbanisation-there are villages inhabited but more remote from the nearest UC. The range has therefore crossed the 40 Km mark in this case. Using this information, the next step was to choose two villages from each remoteness category. The selection procedure for villages kept in view a number of

Table 2
Sample Villages Profile

Village		*Dist Km*	*Area Sq Km*	*Hh No*	*T_POP*	*Np %*	*Service %*	*Mg %*	*Fst %*	*Ag %*
Kamaluwa	Nainital	7	76.00	66	336	40.77	10.12	30.65	0.30	12.50
Lachhampur	Nainital	7	139.00	115	772	3.89	2.98	0.91	0.52	44.43
Jangi Bangar	Nainital	15	61.00	166	724	21.41	10.36	11.05	0.41	8.70
Sitapur	Nainital	18	157.00	102	625	2.56	1.92	0.64	1.92	36.16
Chorgalia	Nainital	25	63.00	45	257	1.17	0.78	0.39	0.00	36.58
Nandhaur	Nainital	26	0.00	119	570	3.57	20.35	3.86	0.53	1.93
Gumaniwala	Dehradun	8	138.00	791	3756	25.67	13.53	12.14	0.96	6.66
Bhattonwala	Dehradun	10	36.02	90	577	7.97	5.89	2.08	0.17	39.51
Kheri Khurd	Dehradun	14	101.17	211	1140	1.24	14.12	3.77	0.35	23.07
Jogiwala Mafi	Dehradun	14	84.99	136	818	0.21	1.71	0.24	0.00	32.03
Timli	Dehradun	28	9906.00	146	592	5.42	32.09	0.00	21.96	11.66
Barkot	Dehradun	37	12192.5	1268	6748	0.10	6.45	1.26	2.45	28.19
Barethi	Uttarkashi	5	140.84	151	885	5.88	5.31	0.56	0.45	44.18
Matli	Uttarkashi	6	380.82	313	1575	11.11	10.92	0.19	0.89	30.54
Hinna	Uttarkashi	12	132.22	218	1610	50.50	50.06	0.43	1.18	3.91
Gajoli	Uttarkashi	14	224.28	88	452	1.33	1.33	0.00	0.00	45.58
Gawana	Uttarkashi	22	97.53	83	347	23.05	23.05	0.00	0.00	30.84
Dang	Uttarkashi	45	158.64	98	466	1.50	1.50	0.00	0.21	43.78

Note: Dist = Distance, Pop = Population, Hh = Household, Np = Non- Primary, Mg = Manufaturing, Fst = Forestry, Ag = Agriculture.

Source: Census 1981 (Village and Town Directory).

considerations. Firstly, an adequate number of households in a village is taken as a minimum condition. Since the proposal is to survey 30 households in each village a cut-off number of 45 households is considered desirable. The feasible villages are then compared in terms of their shares of population engaged in the non-primary sectors, namely manufacturing, trade and services and in the agricultural sector. One village representing a high share in the non-primary sectors and one representing a high share in agriculture is chosen in each case. The village population is stratified by the occupation of the household such as (i) Medium and big farmers (ii) Small and marginal farmers (iii) Artisans (iv) Agricultural and non-farm labourers (v) Self-employed in business, services, household industries etc. (vi) Government employees (vii) Workers in rural unorganized sector and (viii) Others. Using this methodology, from each selected district, six villages were selected at increasing distance from the urban centers where the distance varied from 5 Km to 45 Km. The names of the villages and their profiles based on Census 1981 data are given in Table 4.

Table 3
Selected Villages and Distance from Urban Centre

Village	*Distance Km*	*Village*	*Distance Km*	*Village*	*Distance Km*
Rishikesh		*Haldwani*		*Uttarkashi*	
Gumaniwala	8	Kamalu Gunja Narsingh Talla	7	Bareti	5
Bhuttonwala	10	Lachampur	7	Matli	6
Jogiwala	14	Jangi Bangar	15	Heena	12
Kheri-khurd	14	Sitapur	18	Gajoli	14
Timli	28	Chorgalia Talla Amkhera	25	Ganeshpur	22
Barkot Range	37	Nandaur	26	Dang	45

Source: Census 1981 (Village and Town Directory).

In order to choose the rural households, a random sample of 30 households was drawn from each village giving a total of 180 rural households from around each urban center and 540 households from the rural sector. Thus, a total of 900 households were drawn from the two sectors together. Primary data was collected in June and July of 2004. The overall regional development covering demographic, economic and social aspects of the region was collected from village Pradhan or head of local bodies in urban areas or from responsible authorities. Schedules soliciting information on various social aspects were circulated among the sample households in the rural and urban areas chosen. For analytical purpose, the population was divided in different age groups. These are (i) Small children up to 5 years for health information (ii) Older population above 58 years for health and work (iii) Elementary aged children from 6 to 14 for education (enrolment) (iv) Young adults above 18 years and up to 25 years for education and (v) Adult working age above 25 and up to 58 for educational attainment and employment.

The Selected Clusters

The first cluster is in the district of Dehradun. The geography of the area is partly hilly and the district is highly urbanized with only 49.7% of the population living in rural areas. The literacy rate is relatively poor (69.5%) but there is a concentration of industries, institutes of national importance, etc., in this region. Tourism is an important activity in this area. The urban area is Rrishikesh M.B. This area is in the plains and densely populated. Some of the important sources of employment are (i) services (14.36%) (ii) trade (9.13%) and (iii) manufacturing (6.26%). The rural areas are Gumaniwala, Bhuttanwala, Jogiwala, Kherikhurd, Timli and Barkot range. The topography of the rural areas is partly plain and partly hilly. Some of the important sources of employment in the rural areas are (i) agriculture and forestry (28%) (ii) manufacturing (3%) and (iii) services (11%).

The second cluster is in the district of Nainital. The topography of the area is partly hilly and the district is moderately urbanized with about 67.3% of the population living in rural areas. The literacy rate is poor (56.5%). Main activities in this area are industry, forestry, horticulture and tourism. The urban area in this cluster is Haldwani cum kathgodam M.B which is situated in the plains. Some of the important sources of employment here are: (i) services (14.95%) (ii) trade (8.23%) and (iii) manufacturing (3.96%). The rural areas are Kamalu Gunja, Lachampur, Jangi Bangar, Sita Pur, Chorgalia Talla and Nandaur. The rural areas are completely in the plains. Some of the important sources of employment in the rural area are (i) agriculture and forestry (31%) (ii) manufacturing (8%) and (iii) services (8%).

The third cluster is in the district of Uttarkashi. The topography of the area is completely hilly and the district is almost entirely rural with about 92.83% of the population living in rural areas. The literacy rate is very poor (47.2%). Main activities in this area are agriculture and religious tourism. The urban area in this cluster is Uttarkashi M.B which is situated high in the hills. Some of the important sources of employment here are (i) services (22.44%) (ii) trade (5.37%) and (iii) manufacturing (2.36%). The rural areas are Bareti, Matli, Heena, Gajoli, Ganeshpur and Dang, situated in the hills around Uttarkashi. Some of the important sources of employment in these rural areas are (i) agriculture and forestry (30%) (ii) manufacturing (0.2%) and (iii) services (17.4%).

AN OVERVIEW OF THE SELECTED URBAN AND RURAL CENTRES

Uttarakhand is mostly a rural and agriculture based state but over time, the Census has increasingly included existing villages in the urban classification owing to the growth of the population in these villages. As explained above, from each of the selected urban centres, three wards are considered for the survey, based on their occupational profiles. Many of these urban wards have retained their rural character despite their conversion into urban areas. So the rural urban distinction is blurred in these areas. The urban wards also manifest diverse characteristics often depending on the occupation of the residents and their standards of living. In general the areas with more Government employment or organised business activities are better off in terms of living conditions compared to areas where small traders and labourers resided. The former are found to be conscious of the values of a clean environment, of good quality higher education and complain of the local government's inefficacy and the inadequacies of the local institutes of higher education. However, complaints about the health facilities are common among all residents. Government hospitals, even if they are available, are of little help and the expenditure on medicines is too high. Unemployment is another problem that distresses all classes of people. Primary education and basic facilities like power, water and communication are generally accessible in the urban areas.

The villages are modestly endowed in terms of facilities. In most places, primary school education is available but health facilities are not, creating a serious problem for the rural people. Education facilities are also not adequate beyond the primary level even though the people value higher education. The villages are nearly all electrified but there is a serious problem of drinking water supply. Sometimes rivers and springs are used as sources of drinking water. Bus and Railway stations are usually not nearby and communication is in the form of private vehicles like vans. In Uttarkashi the villages are not easily accessible. Communication problem combines with the inadequacy of facilities to make health care and high-school education difficult. Most of the people in Dehradun and Nainital villages are cultivators as irrigation is easier in these areas, but some work as labourers in other farms. Women are involved in farming and allied activities. Contract jobs in the construction business are common and the business itself is booming as a result of changes in land use from agriculture to other activities. The villages that are closer to the urban centres have much better facilities. In Uttarkashi, agriculture is not very productive due to insufficient irrigation, slopes and encroachment by wild animals. The people depend partly on seasonal tourism. Unemployment is a persistent problem, as the youth do not want to depend on agriculture. New institutions of development are emerging though the Panchayati Raj institution has its problems. The impact of Jawahar Rozgar Yojana (JRY) and the Indira Awaas Yojana (IAY) become evident from the development of approach roads and small low-quality brick houses availed by the poor with free electricity. However, muddy village roads and huts also exist, lending variety to the village scene. The villages enjoy access to communication means like post office and public telephones (Table 4). Dehradun seems to be privileged in respect of other infrastructure.

Selected Wards in the Three Urban Centres

Rishikesh (Dehradun) includes *Ward No. 34*, which is privileged with primary schools, Junior High and High schools and Girls Schools within proximity. There is also a college within 3 Km on Haridwar Road. People are found

Table 4
Access to Village/Urban Infrastructure:Primary Survey

	All weather road access	*Health Facility*	*Transport services*	*Electricity supply*	*Access to post office*	*Public telephone*
Uttarkashi						
Urban Area	1	1	1	Yes	1	1
Bareti	3	2	2	Yes	1	1
Matli	1	3	1	Yes	2	1
Heena	2	1	2	Yes	1	1
Gajoli	2	3	3	Yes	1	2
Ganeshpur	1	1	3	Yes	1	1
Dang	3	2	2	Yes	2	1
Rural Area *	66.67%	66.67%	66.67%	100%	100%	100%
Nainital						
Urban Area	1	1	1	Yes	1	1
Kamalugunja	2	2	3	Yes	2	1
Lachampur	3	2	3	Yes	2	1
Jangi Bangar	1	2	3	Yes	2	1
Sitapur	2	2	3	Yes	2	1
Chorgalia Talla	3	2	3	Yes	2	1

Contd...

	All weather road access	*Health Facility*	*Transport services*	*Electricity supply*	*Access to post office*	*Public telephone*
Nandhaur	2	2	3	Yes	1	1
Rural Area*	66.67%	100%	0%	100%	100%	100%
Dehradun						
Urban Area	1	1	1	Yes	1	1
Gumaniwala	2	1	2	Yes	1	1
Buttonwalla	2	1	3	Yes	2	1
Jogiwala	2	2	2	Yes	1	1
Kherikhurd	1	2	3	Yes	1	2
Timli	2	1	3	Yes	1	1
Barkot range	2	1	3	Yes	2	1
Rural Area*	100%	100%	33.33%	100%	100%	100%
Urban Total*	100%	100%	100%	100%	100%	100%
Rural Total*	77.78%	89%	33.33%	100%	100%	100%

Note: 1-within village or 0 km, 2-within 5 km, 3-access beyond 5 km.

* Rural or Urban access (percentage of centers with facility within 5 km distance, i.e. code 1 or 2)

to aspire for quality education. A Government Hospital is two km. away but a private clinic and a dispensary at nearby Mayakund are perceived more useful though expensive. The people are generally employed in private organisations elsewhere or engaged in private business. Mayakund is another such colony situated on a main road. It has good arrangement for electricity and roadways but water is sometimes a problem. People from other places and states live and work here. The people are mostly labourers working for daily wage or small traders often selling vegetables. The general living standard is low as poverty is high. The area is known for its health facilities including private clinics but the local people find them hard to afford. Government hospital is near at hand but good doctors are lacking and people find it difficult to purchase medicines they are prescribed. People are sometimes forced to resort to home remedies and forego treatment.

Gorakhpur ward in Haldwani (Nainital) is a most advanced colony in Nainital district and is home to many Sikh people who hail from Punjab originally. Social facilities are present but there is complaint of long waiting time and expenses on tests and medicines in the Government hospital. People hold Government jobs or have their own business and shops. Complaints relating to water and power supply are heard as about the high rates of taxes. Tulsinagar is another affluent area where people usually have Government jobs. Basic facilities like electricity and drinking water are available and the location gives the advantage of the main road of Nainital. The usual complaints about Government hospitals remain. People are conscious about cleanliness and the Nagar Palika is subject to the wrath of the people for the poor sanitation provided despite taxes. *Vanbulpura* in contrast is an area with Muslim majority and high levels of poverty. Poverty discourages even children's education in schools. People often seek unqualified doctors' treatment as

Government hospital is inadequate and imposes high cost of medicines. Drinking water is not easily available. Dirty roads and stagnant water blocks speak of the poor sanitation.

The urban people of Uttarkashi municipality (Uttarkashi) are found more satisfied. The *PWD colony* houses mostly labourers and small business holders who have a simple living. The place being a tourist place is clean and bus stand and main Gangotri road help communication. Basic problems of water and electricity are not reported. Primary education is easily accessible but people are concerned about higher education and often children are sent to distant cities for the purpose. Health of the people is ignored because of the expenses. There is no Government hospital nor specialised treatment facility. Ayurveda is commonly used. Natural calamity is a perpetual worry and landslides claim lives. People have to go to Dehradun for emergency. People in this remote area show little interest in Government's working. *Collectorate*, situated on the banks of Ganga is an advanced area in Uttarkashi. People are mostly employed in Government here and people from elsewhere also come for Government service here. Many people live in Government quarters or private houses. Educated and well-qualified people reside here but unemployment is emerging as a serious problem for the youth. Although primary education is not a problem availing higher level education is a problem here and people want technical institutions to come up. Medical care is difficult and costly and good doctors are lacking. The poor allege the presence of discrimination in favour of the well-placed people. There is little faith in the Nagar Nigam for cleanliness and in the Government itself for solving the poorer people's problems. The *Gas Godam colony*, also on the banks of Gangs is in contrast is inhabitated by poorer people who usually have seasonal occupation and often work for wages in tourism activities. Unemployment is a problem. The place is however is situated on the main road and has government departments caring for power, forest and water. Landslide is a serious problem. People show disillusionment with government.

Profiles of Selected Villages

The villages in Dehradun are Gumaniwala, Bhuttonwala, Jogiwala, Kheri Khurd, Timli and Barkot Range. *Gumaniwala* is located along the by pass of Haridwar and is close to Rishikesh urban centre. People of different caste like Brahmin, Rajput schedule caste & schedule tribe dwell in this village. People are generally living below the poverty line. Two canals are present for irrigation and agriculture is the main occupation. Unemployment of youth is a problem. For higher education people go to towns like Rishikesh, Doiwala etc.. There is one primarily school, a junior college and an Anganwadi School in this village. People of this village prefer Rishikesh for medical aid but conveyance is a problem. Communication facilities like Telephone, Postal services are available and water source is Hand Pump. *Bhuttonwala* is 3 Km away from the road between Rishikesh and Haridwar. Access is not easy. Labour, business and Government jobs are common though farming is a dominant occupation with high land productivity. Women are acknowledged to be more educated but they mostly work in fields. The youth seek employment off the farm. There is only one school which is till 5th standard but for higher levels, student have to travel 2 Km away. College is farther away. People travel to Rishikesh for treatment. A.N.M. (Auxiliary Nurse Midwife) works well in this village and there is an Anganwadi. There is a problem of drinking water and people depend upon small canals and water-fall for meeting their daily needs. *Jogiwala* is a village near Dehradun with dense population and developed on urban lines. Most houses are pucca. People from different castes live here. Cultivation has grown less in importance and people hold Government jobs or business. There is one primary and no government-aided school. But private schools are present and college is not far away. There is no Government. Health Centre over here. Government. Hospitals are too far and are crowed. However a private clinic and one Government dispensary cater to people's needs. This village is on the main road between Dehradun and Rishikesh. Market is developed. There is scarcity of drinking water and people get water from tankers. Electricity is a problem. *Kherikhurd* has a population that includes migrants from Garhwal. Half of the population are farmers but rest are wage labourers as land is moving away from cultivation. Village has one primary school and one medical centre with a Government doctor as well as a private clinic. An Anganwadi serves food and provide basic pre-schooling to children. There is no problem in supply of water and electricity. *Timli* is 28 Km from the urban centre and is also surrounded by forest with no other village adjoining. Approximately 300 families reside here and majority of them other than General Caste Hindus. The village has one school up to Class VIII but otherwise all student in the village are in primary schools. The teaching standard is also not impressive. There is hardly any medical facility in the village except a few unqualified doctors. Government or Private clinics are 9 km to 13 km away. It is difficult to cope with any case of emergency. Tube well is used for drinking water and power and voltage are poor quality. Agriculture is hampered by shortage of water as Timli has no river and ground water level is low. The village is however located on the main road. *Barkot,* spread partly in the hills and partly in plains has a total of five hundred households, mostly belonging to General castes. People are a mixed group consisting of government employees, labourers and farmers. Farmers grow mostly rice and wheat in rain fed conditions, as irrigation is a problem. Earning women are numerically more dominant. Village possesses primary school, junior school and inter college. This village does not have any Primary Health Centre. For treatment people go to Doiwala, which is almost 10 Km away. People suffers mainly from cough, cold, fever etc. Villagers prefer private clinics though being expensive but the villagers are satisfied. Lack of drinking water and power are reported and unemployment among educated youth is held as a persistent disappointment.

The villages in Nainital district is Kamalu Gunja, Lachampur, Jangi Bangar, Chorgalia Talla, Sitapur and Nandhaur Range. Kamalu Gunja is widely sprawled village with people belonging to General castes and OBC. Main occupation is farming and young people engage themselves in dairy farming, farming, small business etc. but unemployment is a complaint. The village owns one primary school, one junior high and school, one high school and inter college is near by. Along with this village has one private school up to 12th standard. College is 10 Km away. Health facilities are absent. An Anganwadi is present. *Lachampur* contains households belonging to General and other castes. Agriculture is the main occupation. There is a primary school in the village but there is dissatisfaction with the mid day meal. Medical treatment is a problem and jaundice is common. *Jangi Bangar* has 200 families. Main occupation is farming & labour and people also engage themselves in diary farming, fish rearing, small business etc. Unemployment is also a part of villager's problems. Medical facilities are not present and villagers have to go out of the village for check up and treatment. Unqualified doctor are sometimes known for their medication. Free medication for poor people is an old concept for villagers. Power problem is common affecting irrigation also. Drinking water is taken from tube wells or other wells. People of different communities reside in *Sitapur* and more than 80% are cultivators. Land productivity is high and domestic animals are kept in every house. Unemployment is common. There are primary schools, preparatory schools and for higher education one needs to move out of the village. Unqualified Doctors are famous for home and traditional medication. Government hospitals are not near and are not satisfactory so that people prefer private clinics for medical aid, which is a costly affair. *Chorgalia Talla* is widespread with houses widely separated. Transportation is a problem. Mainly source of income of families' income is through farming. Domestic animals can be seen in every family. Unemployment is the main problem in this village. Private. School, Inter college, Panchyat Bhawan, small market are the main buildings here.. There is a Govt. hospital in proximity but in name only. There are no specialized doctors and neither any female Doctor. People have to wait for long queues for check-up Private clinic is considered. The source of drinking water is from river, which is very harmful for the health of the people. *Nandhaur Range* is farthest from the urban centre. The people belong to General and scheduled castes and are mostly below poverty line. Main occupation of villagers is farming and labour. Govt. hospital is two and a half km away and unqualified doctors are a medical boon. There is one primary school, one girls school and one school up to the standard of 12th within short distance. Drinking water is a problem and people often depend on the river.

The villages in Uttarkashi are Bareti, Matli, Heena, Gajoli, Ganeshpur and Dang. Bareti is close to Uttarkashi. OBC and SC households live along with other castes. Most people are farmers. People complain of irrigation problem and unemployment. Primary and middle school are present but for higher levels children have to travel. Doctors for specific diseases are not available and the village lacks in health facilities. *Matli* is located on the main road to Rishikesh. Most houses are well built. SC households and General castes live here and farming is the main occupation. Rainwater is the main source of farm water though there are rivers at hand which are not utilised. Schools are there at primary and higher levels. The village has Private doctors and a clinic but the expense is too high and facility is inadequate. People go to Uttarkashi in emergencies. The drinking water creates health problems. *Dang* is located on the mountains. Farming is the main occupation though productivity of the soil is not good and rainfall is the source of water. People travel down the hills to get medicine and there is no medical facility in the village. There is one primary school and one girls school near at hand. Gajoli houses people from General castes and SC and people are poor.. There is inequality between Government employees who live here and others. Employment is a problem for labourers. There is a primary school. Getting medical help is a serious problem and people go far for a doctor. For emergency and specialised treatment people go to Dehradun. Water problem is present for irrigation and domestic uses. *Ganeshpur* is on the main road of NH-98. This was affected by the disastrous earthquake of 1991, which affected the living of people in large numbers. After the earthquake this village was renamed as Ganeshpur from Gawana. Government. Jobs or labour are common occupations but people indulge in more than one occupation. Farming is one of them. There is one primary school and a high school is near the village but they are not up to the level of good learning. People send their children out of the village for further education. Education is highly valued. Anganwadi plays an important role in serving the people. There is no health facility except a dispensary. ANM (Auxiliary Midwife, Nurse Mid wife) visits on the monthly basis. In case of emergency people go to Uttarkashi, which is expensive and out of budget of the poor people. Electricity is the main problem in hill station like Gawana. *Heena* is rather inaccessible in the hills. The village was reconstructed after the earthquake. People are engaged in Government. jobs and labour. Agriculture is difficult owing to shortage of water, land sloping and pestilence from wild animals. Women also earn by teaching or self employment programs like vegetable farming, bee-keeping etc. People are mostly below poverty line and unemployment is common. Only one school of primary class is there and for higher studies students have to walk 2 Km away from the village. Fore most problem of this village is of health.

SOCIAL AND ECONOMIC PROFILE OF SAMPLE HOUSEHOLDS

The selected sample has adequate diversity in terms of social composition. The General Category castes dominate the sample followed by OBCs and SCs. ST households were reported in Dang in Uttarkashi. There is a significant Muslim presence in urban Nainital. General Category castes and Hindus are a majority in all areas while non-Hindus are few and found mostly in urban Nainital. OBCs, SCs and STs constitute about 30% to 40% of the sample. The sample household has an average size range of 5.9 to 6.2 in the rural sector and 5.5 to 5.8 in the urban sector, which is close to the NSSO estimation for the state.

The head of the household is usually of married status in the age group 45 to 59 years. Ten per cent or fewer households are female headed and single members (unmarried, divorced or separated) head over 10% of households. On an average, a rural household reported 0.12, 0.09 and 0.11 persons in Dehradun, Nainital and Uttarkashi as migrants (Table 5).

Table 5
Information on Household Head and Household

	Dehradun		*Nainital*		*Uttarkashi*	
Household Head	*Rural*	*Urban*	*Rural*	*Urban*	*Rural*	*Urban*
Model age group (years)	45-59	45-59	45-59	30-44	45-59	45-59
Female (%)	10.8	9.9	10.9	6.7	4.5	9.8
Married (%)	83.0	86.8	84.1	89.2	92.2	33.8
Non-Hindu	10.4	2.5	2.5	27.5	0.8	1.6
General (%)	57.3	76.0	66.1	63.3	68.0	71.3
Migrants per household	0.12	0.03	0.09	0.08	0.11	0.03
Household Size	6.11	5.52	6.20	5.52	5.93	5.79

Source: Author's calculations from Primary Survey.

Table 6
Average Income of Sample Household

Residence	*Sector*	*Dehradun*	*Nainital*	*Uttarkashi*
Number of Income earner (no.)				
Resident	Rural	1.35	1.55	1.21
	Urban	1.53	1.36	1.43
Non-resident	Rural	0.12	0.09	0.11
	Urban	0.03	0.08	0.03
Average Household Income (Rs. per annum)				
Resident	Rural	63336	49538	43464
	Urban	83148	89784	88464
Non-resident	Rural	6432	4188	3876
	Urban	2424	7128	1380
Income per earner (Rs. per annum)				
Resident	Rural	46915	31960	35921
	Urban	54345	66017	61863
Non-resident	Rural	53600	46533	35236
	Urban	80800	89100	46000

Source: Author's calculations from Primary Survey.

The number is lower among urban households, except for Nainital where it is nearly equal. The share of migrant population is lower in the higher age groups. As a phenomenon, it increases with education but is found to be the highest among the school-passed in the Uttarkashi sample. Rural households have more non-resident earners than urban households in all districts and this indicates a greater tendency of rural people to migrate for a livelihood. About 2% to 5% of households do not have any resident income. On an average however, non-resident contribution to household income is meagre with the share being highest in rural Uttarkashi. Resident household income is the biggest part income in all areas (Table 6).

The sample households have numerous sources of income. Households drawing incomes from the modern services sector (cable televisions, repair and IT) and the traditional services sector (teaching and law) are economically better off, especially in urban sector. Since services in general and traditional service in particular require professional education, this implies that professional training pays higher returns to human capital. Most households derive income from non-agricultural employment. Regular/salaried employment is a major source of earning for many households. The income potential vary significantly among the districts. In the sample, the household income is the highest in Nainital and lowest in Uttarkashi (Table 7).

Agro-based enterprises are not found to be profitable in Uttarkashi and Nainital but support high incomes in Dehradun. Salaried jobs, especially government services seem to provide high household incomes relative to other sources, particularly in the rural sector. Households drawing income from non-resident sources receive reasonably high incomes, sometimes higher than from resident sources. Many activities that are supposed to hold great potential like those that are agro-based, timber-based, and in other cottage industries were not found to be of significance in the sample. Services seem to be the leading source of income and enterprises.

Table 7
Household Income (Rs. per month) from Major Sources

	Uttarkashi		*Nainital*		*Dehradun*	
Sources	*Rural*	*Urban*	*Rural*	*Urban*	*Rural*	*Urban*
Agriculture Self-employed	1816	-	3395	84	2907	2675
Agriculture Labour	1811	-	2311	-	1550	-
Agro Based Enterprises	970	-	1500	-	8480	-
Small Shops	1983	2830	2492	5103	3148	4594
Other small business	1916	6325	2761	8432	5818	25255
Traditional Services	3791	7679	3333	9214	6088	4649
Modern Services	1800	5213	4000	5090	2225	3560
Government Services	6500	9071	6617	8053	7374	11188
Other (Salaried) Services	3309	2985	2380	4526	3581	3683
Public Sector	3500	-	-	6000	-	-
Other (large) Industry	2683	-	4267	-	4000	3760
Other Resident Sources	2431	2713	2052	3982	2547	3907
Residential Sources	3622	7372	4128	7482	5278	6929
All sources	3945	7487	4478	8076	5814	7131

Note: Agriculture includes livestock and forestry. Computed for those engaged in the activity only. There may be multiple members earning from different sources in a Household. All sources cover both resident and non-resident incomes.

AGRICULTURE AND RURAL DEVELOPMENT IN SAMPLE VILLAGES

The rural development in Uttarakhand depends critically on the state of agriculture-which is the primary source of rural livelihood-and also on governance, particularly in terms of special development programmes for the villages. Agriculture is the main occupation of the rural people, especially in the rural district of Uttarkashi, where more than 80% of the workforce is engaged in agriculture. For more urbanized Dehradun and Nainital, the share is less (Table 8).

Table 8
Land Use and Agriculture in Dehradun, Nainital and Uttarkashi

Districts	*Agricultural workers %Workforce*	*Net sown area Sq. Km.*	*Gross cropped area Sq. Km.*	*Irrigated area Hectares*	*Rice area Hectares*	*Wheat area Hectares*	*Soyabean area Hectares*	*Fruit Production M.Tonnes*
Uttarkashi	81.0	30975	48774	6241	10050	11811	100	55845
Nainital	68.2	49486	82461	30163	15454	29374	2060	79880
Dehradum	49.3	51002	78065	22461	13621	24191	2	59300

Source: Uttaranchal at a Glance 1999-00.

Among the sample households, the average agricultural area owned is small. It is less than 1 hectare in Uttarkashi and Dehradun but slightly more in Nainital (Table 9). The land is irrigated and most of it is under self-cultivation. Orchards constitute a large part of agricultural land in Dehradun but a small one in Uttarkashi and Nainital. Uttarkashi being highly forested, only 4% of its areas are cultivated leading to a small farm size.

Table 9
Agricultural Land Owned by Households

Districts	*Average Hectare*	*Irrigated %*	*Orchard %*	*Leased-out %*
Uttarkashi	0.26	51.84	2.98	0.58
Nainital	1.04	99.38	1.08	0.00
Dehradun	0.41	80.43	23.45	0.29

Source: Author's calculations from Primary Survey.

Paddy and wheat are the main crops in the state. In the rural sample, paddy was found to be more important and raised in some quantity by most farmers in Uttarkashi and Dehradun followed by wheat, while the rank is reverse in Nainital. Potato, onion and maize are other important crops. Soya bean is a common crop in Nainital. Vegetables and pulses are also commonly grown (Table 10).

Table 10
Crops Raised by Farmers in Order of Importance

Uttarkashi	*Nainital*	*Dehradun*
Paddy	Wheat	Paddy
Wheat	Paddy	Wheat
Potato	Maize	Chari
Mandua	Tomato	Green Vegetables
Onion	Soyabean	Maize
Ramdana	Chana	Grass
Mustard	Fodder	Sugarcane
Urad	Sugarcane	Dal
Rajma	Mustard	Bajra

Source: Author's calculations from Primary Survey.

A very large section of cultivators raise rice and wheat, especially in Uttarkashi where a large share of households raises both staples. Maize and soya bean are found to be a choice mostly among Nainital households while the Uttarkashi sample did not contain households growing sugarcane. The average yield rate of rice and wheat in the sample (for the three districts) is lower than the reported national and state averages (Table 11), but the yield of rice in Dehradun and soyabean in Nainital are found to be high.

Table 11
Yield Rates of Some Common Crops (100 kg/ hectares)

Crop	*Uttar-kashi*	*Naini-tal*	*Dehra-dun*	*3-Districts (mean)*	*Uttara-khand*	*India*
Rice	13.0	14.6	22.2	15.6	19.9	19.13
Wheat	12.2	16.1	16.7	15.5	20.2	27.4
Maize	2.5	9.12	9.1	9.2	13.1	18.4
Soyabean	4.2	11.3	-	11.3	6.9	8.2
Sugarcane	-	385.4	352	380	612.5	696.4

Source: Govt. of Uttarakhand, India and Author's calculations from Primary Survey.

The small cultivator has a higher yield for rice and wheat compared to the combined sample in Uttarkashi, but in other cases there is not much evidence of an inverse influence of scale (Table 12a). Wheat is mostly raised in irrigated areas and while other crops are raised in both irrigated and rainfed areas. More than 80% of the households raise wheat in all the three districts but in Nainital paddy is grown by about 72% of the households. Paddy and wheat are preferred in Uttarkashi where the percentages of households are 93 and 96 respectively and the small farmers do not show any special bias towards these conventional crops.

Table 12a
Cultivation by Households

	Uttarkashi		*Nainital*		*Dehradun*	
	Sm Cu	*Total*	*Sm Cu*	*Total*	*Sm Cu*	*Total*
Wheat Cultivators						
%of cultivating Households	92.80	92.90	92.60	93.20	82.90	83.60
Total Area (hect/household)	0.20	0.26	0.76	0.98	0.46	0.50
Total yield (Quint/hect)	15.40	12.19	14.87	16.12	16.37	16.72
Irrigated area (hect/household)	0.15	0.20	0.60	0.85	0.37	0.40
Irrigated yield (Quint/hect)	16.25	12.45	18.62	18.40	20.35	21.08
Paddy Cultivators						
%of cultivating Households	95.70	95.70	71.90	71.60	81.40	82.10
Total Area (hect/household)	0.19	0.24	0.70	0.76	0.38	0.42
Total yield (Quint/hect)	24.89	19.54	15.19	21.95	34.97	33.37
Irrigated area (hect/household)	0.15	0.19	0.40	0.50	0.33	0.35
Irrigated yield (Quint/hect)	31.08	24.31	26.57	33.49	38.87	39.28
Maize Cultivators						
%of cultivating Households	1.0	0.90	59.50	56.80	6.20	6.00
Total Area (hect/household)	0.07	0.07	0.68	0.70	0.19	0.19
Total yield (Quint/hect)	2.5	2.5	8.20	9.12	9.10	9.10
Irrigated area (hect/household)	0.08	0.08	.87	.95	.47	.47
Irrigated yield (Quint/hect)	0.03	0.03	0.35	0.38	0.19	0.19

Note: Sm Cu = Small Cultivators.
Source: Author's calculations from Primary Survey.

Soyabean is a preferred crop in Nainital (Table 12b), grown by the small farmers and others but 14% of farmers in Dehradun also raise soyabean. Irrigated yield is slightly higher in small farms in Nainital. A small section of farmers grow sugarcane in Nainital and Dehradun but they are mostly medium or large farmers.

Table 12b
Cultivation by Households

	Uttarkashi		*Nainital*		*Dehradun*	
	Sm Cu	*Total*	*Sm Cu*	*Total*	*Sm Cu*	*Total*
Soyabean Cultivators						
%of cultivating Households	2.40	2.40	40.50	43.20	11.80	14.00
Total Area (hect/household)	0.06	0.06	0.91	0.91	0.00	0.00
Total yield (Quint/hect)	4.22	4.22	11.18	11.34		
Irrigated area (hect/household)	0.05	0.05	0.78	0.76	0.00	0.00
Irrigated yield (Quint/hect)	8.96	8.96	12.95	13.75		
Sugarcane Cultivators						
%of cultivating Households	0.00	0.00	0.00	6.10	3.10	6.00
Total Area (hect/household)	0.00	0.00	1.17	1.66	2.42	1.28
Total yield (Quint/hect)			249.7	385.45	338.0	352.1
Irrigated area (hect/household)	0.00	0.00	0.85	1.37	2.02	1.03
Irrigated yield (Quint/hect)			343.4	466.59	400.0	440.9

Note: Sm Cu = Small Cultivators.
Source: Author's calculations from Primary Survey.

In the sample, it is found that agriculture is no longer the main source of earning, as the income potential is limited in this activity. Rural people take recourse to other economic activities, especially construction and other services for additional income. In fact, less than 25% of sample households reported agriculture (as self employed or labour) as the largest source of household income.

Regular employment (Government or private) is found to be much more profitable in the sample. Agriculture income is found to be more important in Nainital and least in Uttarkashi.

Uttarakhand, like most states in India, has several rural development programmes. The Jawahar Rozgar Yojana and the food for work programmes (Table 13) are most prominent in Uttarkashi while they are least prominent in Nainital. Although the programmes have led to creation of community roads, the fund is inadequate making their reach rather small. The IRDP also plays a sizable part in these programmes, but in terms of benefits to the poor, their impact has dwindled. While there are provisions for old age and widow pensions, they are strongly criticized, as most needy people cannot avail them due to strict eligibility conditions, inadequate amounts and irregular payments. Scholarship schemes have helped education to an extent but they are restricted to primary levels. Higher education has been hampered by inadequate transport facilities to urban areas. The contribution of the Indira Awaas Yojana to the poor is evident in the pucca houses but this programme too has run into fund problem. The electrification of the villages has been a success but power supply is poor. Many villages have inadequate water supply and water used for drinking and cooking is often collected from rivers and lakes. Health problems are most acute in these areas. People from most rural areas have to travel large distances, by vans or other private vehicles, to avail health facilities, which in most cases are of low quality. Private sector participation is a positive sign in the field of health and education. Private medical clinics have started coming up in these areas. Private 'English Medium' schools are also common in these areas, as rural people prefer them, expecting higher quality education. Although this phenomenon appears to be successful, these facilities are found to be expensive.

Table 13
Percentage of Household Benefited by Rural Development Programmes

Govt. Programmes	*Uttarkashi*	*Nainital*	*Dehradun*
Jawahar Rojgar Yojna	31.4	1.3	5.8
Food For Work Programme	12.0	0.4	0.8
EAS	0.4	0.4	0.0
IRDP	7.4	10.0	5.8
DWCRA	0.8	0.4	0.0
TRYSEM	1.7	0.8	0.0
PMRY	5.7	1.3	1.3
Old Age Pension	7.3	3.4	5.0
Widow Pension	8.6	5.0	7.9
Rural Scholarship	14.8	18.8	15.8
Free Text Book Scheme	25.3	18.8	18.7
Jal Dhara	11.0	21.3	12.5

Source: Author's calculations from Primary Survey.

Every village has a Panchayat as the local government. Community participation has increased with the emergence of women's groups and their activities. The sample households recognize the help imparted by these organizations. The status of women and their empowerment also seem to have improved by this participation. The financial infrastructure is underdeveloped in these areas. People show preference to moneylenders and women's organization for credit than to formal banks.

Gaps in Rural Development from the Villager's Viewpoint

The rural millions in India have been traditionally described as fatalistic. In the 1960s this had been viewed as a stumbling block for agriculture development. However, this view was proved wrong as technology and enterprise led to a flourishing green revolution. However, deprivation in terms of human development remained in rural areas. Education and health-care remained primitive. The rural population faced poor housing conditions, lack of sanitation and minimum supply of modern amenities. Recent development paradigms have however stressed changes in these conditions, as facilities that were earlier associated with an urban life have now become part of rural development plans. Poverty alleviation plans now ensure that even the poor in the rural areas have some access to proper house, electricity, water, education and health.

In the sample, people from almost all villages were unanimous in complaining of two shortfalls in development, i.e., employment and health. They no longer accept agriculture as a way of life and look for productive employment beyond this sector. Most of them were disappointed that there was not enough non-farm employment available in the region. They also felt the need for adequate health facilities in the village. Unemployment is a burning problem in the rural regions of Uttarakhand and the people in the sample who were interviewed expressed their anguish at the inadequacy of job opportunities. Young men mentioned their aversion to agriculture and expressed their preference for self-employment rather than regular salaried jobs. They appreciated the need for such jobs while utilizing the institution of self help groups. Difficulty in getting bank loans was voiced as another constraint to self-employment. Women's need for training in relevant activities was also expressed. The sample villages are full of enterprising and aspiring women-mostly educated-ready to engage in some productive activity in their own areas. They demanded better marketing facilities for pursuing profitable trades. In the absence of other remunerative activities, these women are forced into subsistence agriculture. Nearly all villages in the sample complained of the existing public health facilities. They felt that their localities should have health centers and existing health centers should have improved facilities. They also wanted better quality service, experienced doctors and proper medicines. Some villages complained of inadequate water supply, both for consumption and irrigation. Apart from these, in some villages there are problems of pests and wild animals and people expressed the need for fencing against these animals. In other villages, farmers complained of the lack of training on organic farming methods and use of bio-fertilizers.

6

SOCIAL AND ECONOMIC DISPARITY: EVIDENCES FROM PRIMARY SURVEY

This chapter brings to light the situation on the ground as actually experienced and perceived by the people and relates to their economic as well as social well-being. We have already discussed in chapter five (see Table 5.7) that there is clear indication of rural urban disparity in terms of household incomes. This is further reinforced by the finding that those sources that are significant to the rural people (self employed in agriculture, agricultural labour, agro-based enterprises etc.) have much lower income potential than other sources of income. The subjects taken up are (1) Employment as a most important concern impinging on the standards and dignity of living of people, (2) Education as an enabling factor and a route to meaningful employment and empowerment, (3) Health care as an essential facility of life and an instrument that enables one to work productively and (4) Physical amenities, that as a group, defines the quality of life and the participation in progress that human community is achieving on a wider front.

EMPLOYMENT

One of the important responsibilities of a state is to create an environment where people who seek gainful employment get them. This enables them to lead their life with dignity and contributes to social cohesion. The state seeks to facilitate this process by making education accessible to all. However, education also creates a craving for employment that gives higher remunerations. Clearly, if the creation human resources is not consistent with the demands of the economic system, it can lead to much social unrest. We find from our survey that the employment situation in Uttarakhand has given rise to such a situation, particularly in the rural areas of the state.

Agriculture has traditionally been the main source of work in rural Uttarakhand. However, for a majority of the rural populace considered to be engaged in agriculture, this is a delusion due to the low returns from this sector. Today, the youth is hardly satisfied with a life in agriculture, and consider it equivalent to unemployment. Thus, the lack of quality employment opportunities has led to a feeling of unrest among the rural youth. This applies to a certain extent to the urban youth as well, but the household survey found a stark urban bias as far as employment opportunities are concerned.

The survey categorizes employment in the working age (above 25 years) into various groups that vary mainly in terms of the security of their employment status. The minimum working age considered here takes into consideration the time needed by an individual to complete his or her education together with some search time that is often necessary to obtain satisfactory employment. This is in contrast to conventional categorization such as the cut-off age 15 considered by NSSO. The definition of 'unemployed' is based on an individuals' perception about his or her own employment status. Similarly, the 'self-employed' category is also recorded by their self-declaration. Many people-mostly women-work at home, field or other enterprises without drawing remuneration. We have classified such people as unpaid family workers wherever they have identified themselves as such (as distinct from self-employed or unemployed) without attempting any distinction between market based and other forms of work.

Table 1
Employment Status(%) of Adult Working Age-Group (26-58)

	Total		*Female*	
	Rural	*Urban*	*Rural*	*Urban*
Dehradun				
Unemployed	12.5	6.4	3.0	0.0
Casual	6.9	4.6	2.0	0.0
Part-Time Job	2.5	1.8	0.3	0.8
Temporary Salaried	8.1	10.4	1.0	0.0
Regular Salaried (Full Time)	10.5	12.1	3.4	1.5
Self Employed	16.0	21.4	5.4	5.4
Unpaid family worker	43.4	43.2	84.9	92.3
Nainital				
Unemployed	11.6	4.8	0.7	1.5
Casual	8.3	10.0	4.8	3.0
Part-Time Job	0.9	0.7	0.4	0.8
Temporary Salaried	5.7	7.8	1.9	1.5
Regular Salaried (Full Time)	6.4	9.3	0.4	1.5
Self Employed	26.2	23.3	10.0	2.3
Unpaid family worker	40.8	44.1	81.8	89.5
Uttarkashi				
Unemployed	11.6	9.1	0.4	0.0
Casual	9.8	3.1	3.2	0.7
Part-Time Job	1.8	0.7	0.0	0.7
Temporary Salaried	3.2	4.9	0.4	2.2
Regular Salaried (Full Time)	13.8	19.9	4.0	5.8
Self Employed	13.8	19.9	3.2	3.6
Unpaid family worker	46.0	41.6	88.8	85.6

Note: The numbers may not add up to 100 because other employment categories namely, retired with pension, retired with no pension, old/child and student are not reported in this table.
Source: Author's calculations from Primary Survey.

In the sample, self-employment is the most dominant category in paid employment, in both rural and urban sectors. In the rural sector this reflects the importance of cultivation on owned land. Tourism, travel, processing and packaging activities relating to agro-products account for the high share of self-employed in urban as well as rural sectors. The share of self-employed is 26% in Nainital, 16% in Dehradun and 14% in Uttarkashi in the rural sector and 23%, 21% and 20% respectively in the urban. In the rural sector, the unemployed comes next in share in Dehradun and Nainital but in Uttarkashi self-employed and regular employed are the important status along with unemployment. In the urban sector regular employment is most common (after unpaid employment) in Uttarkashi and Dehradun but casual and self employments are more important in Nainital. Unemployment is less in urban areas, accounting for 6%, 5% and 9% of the working age population respectively in Dehradun, Nainital and Uttarkashi compared to about 12% in the rural parts.

In all the three districts the share of unemployed is significantly larger in the rural sector than in the urban sector. Not only this, casual and the part-time jobholders constitute a higher share in the rural sector in Dehradun and Uttarkashi. On the other hand, the urban people enjoy more of the secure and salaried jobs, both temporary and regular. Even with respect to self-employment, the urban sector does better though both sectors show this incidence in Nainital. These clearly reflect the rural urban disparity in terms of job opportunities relative to the aspirations in Uttarakhand.

Among women, a large part of the population in the working age group (not less than 80%) declared themselves as unpaid family workers, who work in both the household and the market. Needless to say, such services may have economic value but are not valued by any accounting procedure. Among men, the share of this category is extremely small. It is however notable that the share of unpaid workers is more among urban women in Dehradun and Nainital, the two districts that are more in the plains and are more urbanised. The share of unemployed is higher among rural women who appear to be more prepared for work outside their households than their urban counterparts.

Within self-employment, there does not seem to be any urban bias with respect to females. In fact in Nainital, 10% of the female population in the working age group are self-employed in the rural sector compared to 2% in the urban sector. Certain entrepreneurial and marketing skill promotion can lead to more of such mass self-employment. Women's participation in economic life in Uttarakhand is clear from the emerging importance of women's organizations. Some households were found to be depending on the woman for arranging credit for small businesses and for making financial contributions to the family. Women's education and employment are encouraged in these households.

Conventionally, education through schooling and university-based higher studies was expected to make a person employable. However, this ceases to be an effective process in a world where technical skills are required. In India, with the State moving away from production related activities, it is the private sector that is expected to fill up the gap, fulfilling the crucial task of employment generation. The State meanwhile facilitates business and the employment opportunities by promoting the kind of skills the business needs. Vocational training and entrepreneurial training given to men and women can help employment and self-employment in such circumstances. Self-employment opportunities are particularly useful for women who seek flexibility to synchronize work with household responsibilities. Skills in computer usage are useful in a world undergoing an information technology revolution, and this should provide a big opportunity to a remote state like Uttarakhand. Vocational skills can lead to increased demand for jobs or self-employment opportunities. The aspirations increase and people look for more skilled and higher paid jobs than they did earlier. As a result more people are likely to perceive themselves unemployed. The nature and quality of the skills have to be designed carefully failing which, unemployment among skilled population will create disillusion about the programmes. Finally, creation of skills and human resource development is not enough. Development of adequate infrastructure, credits, marketing facility and market information and upgradation of skills are essential for making use of the training and simultaneous creation of demand in the labour market.

Examining the profiles of the various trained categories, we with computer training with at least ten years education are likely to declare themselves as unemployed. The survey does not find people with vocational training and incomplete schooling to be unemployed, except in rural Dehradun and Uttarkashi. Interestingly, this educational profile is associated with only regular employment or unemployment in rural Uttarkashi. Those with the training and complete schooling are likely to be regular employees in the urban sector. However, vocational training with no schooling has not proved useful. Unemployment is also high among general graduates (college degree) with no training. It is as high as 33% in Uttarkashi and least in Nainital. There is clear rural urban disparity as there is a greater incidence of unemployment in rural areas among people with 10 years schooling and training. Of the rural people with class 10 education and a vocational training, 42%, 35% and 27% are unemployed in the rural sector and 9%, 16% and 4% in the urban sector. The disparity is evident even with the computer-trained people, except in Uttarkashi. Thus, there is a need to develop opportunities for the trained and the skilled in rural areas.

Table 2
Employment Status (%) Among Recipients of Education and Training

		Vocational training			
	Graduate with no vocational or computer training %	*10 year school %*	*< 10 year school %*	*No-school %*	*Computer training With complete schooling*
Dehradun					
Rural					
Unemployed	22.8	42.3	22.2	25.0	48.3
Regular salaried	17.8	11.5	11.1	0.0	6.9
Self employed	10.9	15.4	11.1	0.0	3.4
Urban					
Unemployed	24.0	9.4	0.0	0.0	17.4
Regular salaried	14.0	18.8	0.0	0.0	21.7
Self employed	14.0	12.5	50.0	0.0	34.8
Nainital					
Rural					
Unemployed	11.3	35.0	–	100.0	30.0
Regular salaried	12.9	5.0		0.0	15.0
Self employed	21.0	25.0		0.0	5.0
Urban					
Unemployed	12.2	15.8	–	0.0	17.1
Regular salaried	14.6	23.7		0.0	28.6
Self employed	26.8	7.9		0.0	8.6
Uttarkashi					
Rural					
Unemployed	32.8	27.3	50.0	0.0	11.1
Regular salaried	12.5	27.3	50.0	0.0	11.1
Self employed	7.8	9.1	0.0	0.0	33.3
Urban					
Unemployed	32.8	3.7	0.0	0.0	18.2
Regular salaried	13.1	51.9	0.0	0.0	27.3
Self employed	16.4	14.8	0.0	0.0	0.0

Source: Author's calculations from Primary Survey.

Ironically, graduation (university education) and computer training are important in fetching regular employment, but are also instrumental in pushing up aspirations for better jobs. These categories thus lead both in terms of unemployment and regular employment. Some education and vocational or computer training is always found useful for self-employment. However, the quality as well as availability of training institutes is inadequate. Besides, the rural sector is yet to be adequately developed to absorb the trained manpower. Promotion of self-employment will be essential in the coming days.

EDUCATION

Education can build up a generation with desirable social and economic qualities, capabilities and an ingrained balanced attitude to gender. Education of women in particular will help in removing the age-old gender discrimination noted in the secondary analysis also, empower women and pave the way to a more enlightened and capable future generation besides utilizing women power for economic development. In light of the fact that education has remained in an undeveloped state and even the literacy level was far from satisfactory, the government in India put emphasis on primary and elementary education from the beginning and in particular in the 1990s.

Literacy and Schooling

In Uttarakhand, secondary data indicated an improvement in literacy rates and a significant expansion in school infrastructure. The rural urban gap exists but the rural sector showed commendable performance. The village schedules in our survey revealed reasonable access to primary education. However, access to higher education does not match people's expectations. Table 3 based on the survey data gives a mixed picture as far as rural urban disparity in the incidence of non-schooled population is concerned. However, this result is based on the data that has been pooled across ages, which might be misleading as they do not reveal the impact of past failures and recent achievements separately. We have therefore also looked at the outcome of the attempts by exploring the achievements in (i) drawing the population towards school education, (ii) retention and the successful completion of the process.

Table 3
Non-Schooled (%) Members in Sample Households

District	*All*		*Females*	
	Rural	*Urban*	*Rural*	*Urban*
Uttarkashi	30.1	19.10	41.8	25.1
Nainital	25.6	28.7	33.4	33.0
Dehradun	28.2	18.2	36.5	23.5

Note: Rates are for all age groups.
Source: Author's calculations from Primary Survey.

Education in Adult Age Group

In the first approach mentioned above, the data includes only the age groups beyond the school age in order to capture the success of the measures and improvement over generation. Two successive age groups are considered, i.e., the young adults (19 to 25 years) and the adult working age group (26 to 58 years). Comparison is made between the percentages of population in the age groups with (a) no schooling and (b) schooling completed (Madhyamik and above). The former throws light on the achievement of minimum schooling. The latter relates to the achievement of continual and successful completion. Table 4, summarising the school achievements based on the sample supports the secondary based finding that education has indeed spread over time in the three districts in both rural and urban sectors. However, even after such substantial achievements in the rural sector, this sector still lags behind the urban sector in Dehradun and Uttarkashi.

The younger age group shows much higher percentages compared its older counterpart in terms of both 'no schooling' and 'schooling completed' although females fall behind males on both counts. The younger generation shows remarkable ability for catching up, especially in rural areas. In fact in Nainital, the rural population fared better than their urban counterparts in the 'no schooling' category. As mentioned earlier, the rural urban gap is found to exist in Dehradun and Uttarkashi, but with diminishing tendency over the generations. The percentage for higher education also shows similar results. The rural women show high attainment rates in terms of school education and higher education that are higher than those for men in some cases. The share of women with 'schooling completed' is higher than the share of the total population in the young adult group for Dehradun and Nainital.

Table 4
Educational Attainments (%)

Age group	*Dehradun*		*Nainital*		*Uttarkashi*	
	No schooling	*School complete*	*No schooling*	*School complete*	*No schooling*	*School complete*
Rural						
Total						
19–25	10.8	66.4	5.7	66.9	9.4	68.9
26–58	31.2	41.7	26.7	36.7	32.6	35.9
Female						
19–25	10.1	68.8	8.5	68.8	16.7	59.7
26–58	47.5	23.1	41.7	18.9	57.8	18.4
Urban						
Total						
19–25	9.1	71.7	23.8	56.0	1.8	87.3
26–58	18.4	52.2	27.4	52.4	16.3	49.6
Female						
19–25	10.6	66.0	32.5	42.5	1.9	84.6
26–58	30.4	37.6	33.9	50.0	28.6	53.2

Source: Author's calculations from Primary Survey.

In the adult working age group, there is a wide rural urban gap where urban sector is ahead in minimum education and also higher school education. Dehradun is the most advanced district among rural regions in 'school completed' criterion while Uttarkashi is the most backward of the three. In Nainital, the urban sector seems to be lagging behind the rural sector and this calls for some attention to this area.

Graph 1
Education of adult age (26-58) Dehradun, Nainital and Uttarakashi

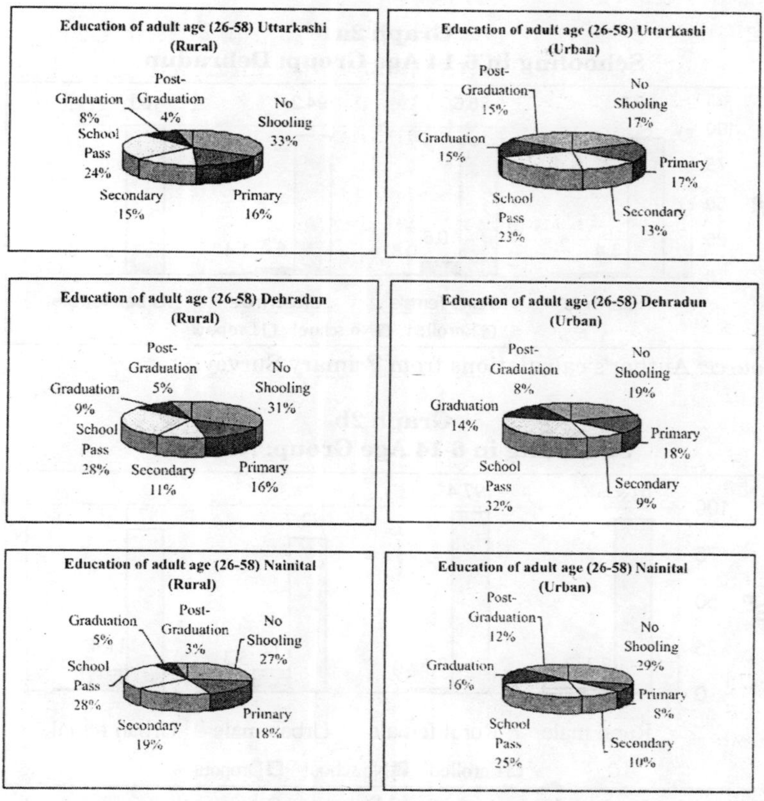

Source: Author's calculations from Primary Survey.

Elementary Schooling Age Group

From the sample, the age group between 6 and 14 years is examined in order to analyze the success of elementary schooling in the state. The share of this age group enrolled in schools is very high with more than 90% rates in all districts and for both genders. Drop out rates for those who have once been to school, is extremely low and is perceptible only for males in urban Nainital. However, the share of those who have never gone to school is of concern as this is larger than the share of drop outs in all districts, and is largest for females in rural Dehradun:

Graph 2a
Schooling in 6-14 Age Group: Dehradun

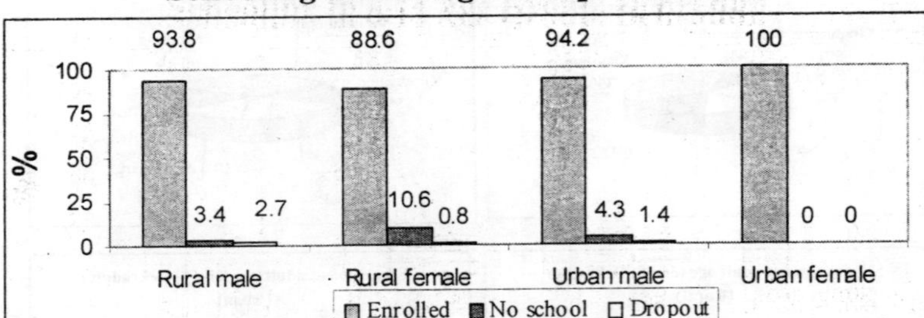

Source: Author's calculations from Primary Survey.

Graph 2b
Schooling in 6-14 Age Group: Nainital

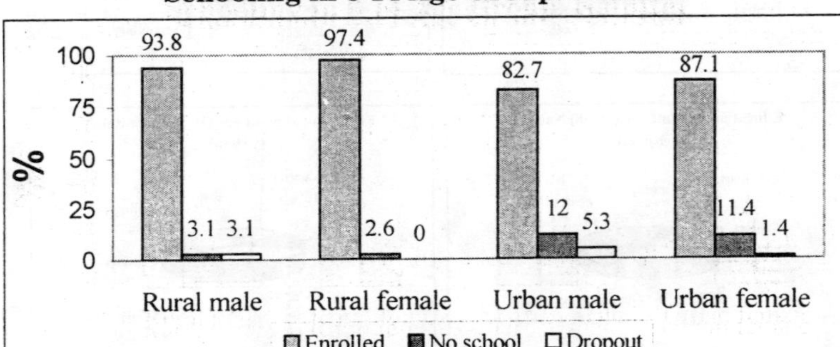

Source: Author's calculations from Primary Survey.

Graph 2c
Schooling in 6-14 Age Group: Uttarakashi

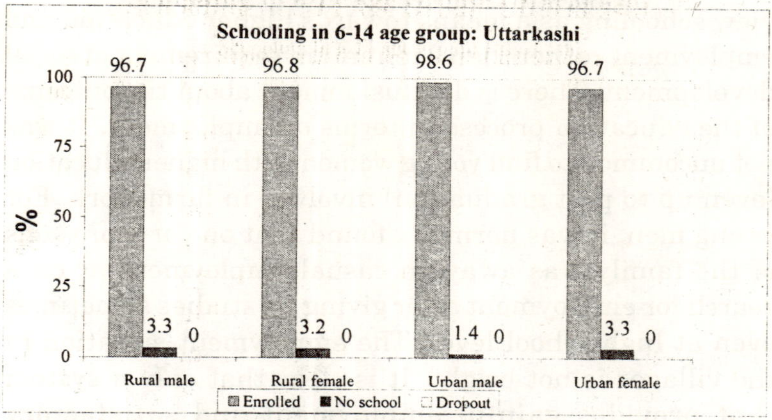

Source: Author's calculations from Primary Survey.

Village wise Analysis

There is significant variation in the educational performance of the villages. There is a slight tendency of the educational indicators of the villages to improve with their nearness to the urban centre. There are however exceptions such as Barkot in Dehradun, that have fared commendably despite the distance from the urban centre. In Uttarkashi, remote villages like Ganeshpur and Dang have achieved a lot in terms of educational performance. Uttarkashi shows relatively better diffusion of development in terms of school education. The spread of school education in rural areas has been associated with the construction of schools within short distances while the spread of higher education is a result of the growth of distance education. In this context, households complained of commutation difficulties that hampered the continuance of education, especially for girls for whom, security is a major concern. There is evidence of this gender imbalance in every district. Considering the working age group, i.e., 26 to 58, women exceed men in 'no schooling' category and fall short in the 'school completed' criteria. People view schooling as a means towards higher education and employment rather than a minimum requirement of social development. There is disillusionment about the outcome of the education process in terms of employment. It was not uncommon to find young women with higher education (even up to post graduation) involved in farm work. For young men, it was normally found that one or more sons of the family was away on casual employment or on a search for employment after giving up studies sometimes even at high school level. The employment situation in the villages is not bright. It is clear that only a system that provides gainful employment and satisfactory earning opportunities to the people can go a long way in making sustained education possible and meaningful to the people.

Cost of School Education

Expenditure on sending a child to school is one of considerations that may affect educational achievements from the demand side. On the average schooling is found to cost between Rs. 1500 to Rs. 2400 in the rural areas, and higher in the urban areas ranging from Rs. 3000 to Rs. 3600. While government schools are commonly selected, many households chose private schools for their children. The cost is lowest in Dehradun in both rural and urban sectors and the cost is highest in Uttarkashi among the rural people and in Nainital in the urban areas. The high cost of Nainital urban area may be related to its meagre achievement in the education front. Traveling time is also a cost and traveling is found to be more time consuming in the rural areas except in Uttarkashi where the time taken is same for the two sectors. The students receive scholarships and the amount is highest in urban Uttarkashi.

Table 5
Average Cost of Education

	Dehradun		*Nainital*		*Uttarkashi*	
	Rural	*Urban*	*Rural*	*Urban*	*Rural*	*Urban*
Expenditure (Rs/year)	1492	2788	2087	3652	2394	3126
Travel time (hours)	0.9	0.6	0.9	0.6	0.7	0.7
Scholarship (Rs/year)	408	314	452	347	381	1065

Source: Author's calculations from Primary Survey.

HEALTH SCENARIO

The secondary information throws limited light on the health facilities of Uttarakhand. RCH data, which throw some limited light, only, clearly indicate that much needs to be done. During the survey, the rural and urban people uniformly complained about the miserable state of health facility in the state. In general the health situation has two considerations. (1) The health situation reflecting the preventive side is important. A clean environment, hygienic conditions, awareness, vaccination and suitable food habits can avoid most diseases. The cost of bad health is well known. Illness means days lost which reflects on earnings and family well being. Expenditure in monetary terms is a burden and anxiety is involved. It also means loss of productivity. Added to this is the external effect as many diseases are infectious. The preventive responsibility falls on a wide domain of public health and civic organizations, general education and economic well being. (2) The curative side is the responsibility of the health departments. Private sector partnership can also help but often proves more expensive. A well performing health sector will provide access to health facilities and minimize cost especially to the poor. The survey therefore enquires about incidences of illness, treatment and cost as also civic amenities that influence health and quality of life. Information on health facilities available are provided in the village and UC descriptions.

The overview of the sample rural and urban centers showed that the selected villages mostly complained about the lack of health centers and even traveling to the nearest hospital was said to be cumbersome. Even that does not always help since there is lack of good doctors and facilities anyway. Purchasing medicine also proves costly. For emergency people have to go far. In many cases people take the services of private facilities as available, but expense proves to be a problem for the basic privilege. When trained help is not available, villagers take recourse to non-qualified and indigenous facilities. The ICDS Anganwadis are reported to be of more help in case of child health. The urban case is no better. The urban people also find the facilities lacking badly and have similar complaints. Due to population distribution the incidence of illness if naturally biased towards the rural sector accounting more than 65% of cases (Graph 3).

Graph 3
Composition of the Ill People by Residence

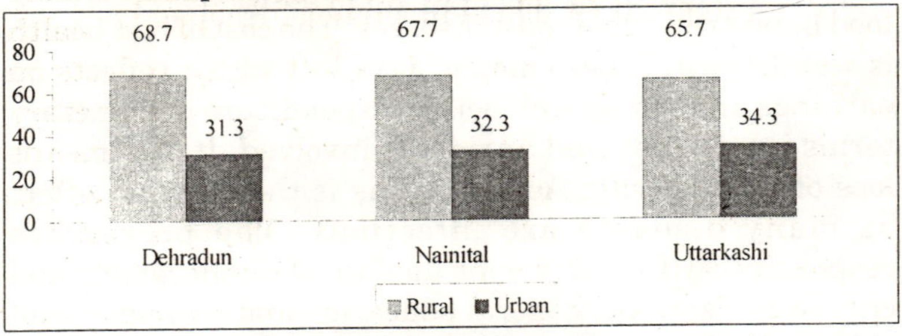

Source: Author's calculations from Primary Survey.

The survey identifies the main diseases afflicting people in the areas. Fever presumably of viral origin is the most common illness followed by cough and cold. Infant illness is also a problem. Dysentery and Diarrhea are important diseases constituting 14 to 15% of the diseased in Dehradun and Uttarkashi but in Nainital the incidence is uncommon. Among infectious diseases pneumonia and malaria affected people but their incidence relatively was less and mostly confined to rural Dehradun and urban Uttarkashi. It is also noted that among common diseases, sources of some diseases are not known specifically in rural areas. This probably speaks of the diagnostic inadequacy in rural areas. The greater prevalence of anemia in urban areas may have a similar diagnostic reason. Problems of pregnancy are more common in rural areas. (Table 6).

Table 6
Common Diseases and Percentage of Persons Ill

	Dehradun		*Nainital*		*Uttarkashi*	
Name of Disease	*Rural*	*Urban*	*Rural*	*Urban*	*Rural*	*Urban*
Diarrhoea	6.8	4.1	1.6	2.0	3.3	3.3
Dysentry	7.3	11.6	3.9	1.3	11.1	8.5
Cough and Cold	16.4	26.2	17.2	16.4	10.5	25.5
Fever (Viral)	20.6	16.9	29.8	30.3	27.5	17.0
Malaria	1.4	1.7	0.6	0.7	0.3	3.3
Pneumonia	2.8	0.6	0.3	0.0	1.0	0.0
Problems of Teeth	1.7	1.2	1.0	0.0	1.3	2.0
Anaemia or Weakness	2.3	5.8	1.9	2.6	2.0	4.6
Pain in stomach	4.8	2.3	4.5	0.0	10.8	0.7
Fracture	1.4	0.6	0.6	1.3	1.0	1.3
Specifically Women related diseases	0.8	0.6	0.6	0.0	1.3	0.7
Complications in women related to pregnancy and child birth	2.5	0.6	2.6	2.0	3.0	0.7
Problems of new born baby	10.2	12.2	6.1	12.5	0.7	11.8
Disease not known	2.0	0.0	2.3	0.0	2.6	0.0

Note: Based on the last 3 months' information.
Source: Author's calculations from Primary Survey.

Comparing the number of days ill, Uttarkashi shows the least duration of illness on average and no particular pattern of rural urban difference emerges. There is a gender difference and the females are ill longer in rural areas than males and similar direction is reported in urban (Table 7). The average time duration of illness of a person was found higher in rural sector than urban in Dehradun, nearly same in Uttarkashi but less in Nainital. The result is similar gender wise for Dehradun and Nainital. In Nainital both male and female were reported ill for longer duration in urban areas. More relevantly, the number of days of illness per person is highest for the older (above 58 years) population in the rural areas in all cases. The duration also rises with age in urban Dehradun and Nainital. Among younger children (1-5 years) no disparity is evident in Dehradun but in Nainital and Uttarkashi the duration in urban areas is more.

Table 7
Mean Number of Days Ill of Sample Population in Last 6 Months

	Dehradun			*Nainital*			*Uttarkashi*		
Rural	*M*	*F*	*T*	*M*	*F*	*T*	*M*	*F*	*T*
0-5	1.0	1.4	1.2	2.2	1.8	2.0	3.5	1.1	2.4
6-58	5.0	6.5	5.7	3.9	5.6	4.7	3.1	4.7	3.9
>58	20.7	28.7	23.9	19.4	14.0	16.4	9.7	11.6	10.6
All	5.9	7.3	6.6	4.7	5.9	5.3	3.7	4.8	4.3
Urban									
0-5	.5	2.0	1.1	4.9	7.5	6.0	10.6	0.9	6.8
6-58	3.9	6.6	5.7	7.2	6.0	4.7	3.3	4.9	3.9
>58	5.1	12.8	8.7	12.5	30.8	19.5	3.6	2.2	2.9
All	3.7	6.7	5.1	7.2	7.3	7.3	4.2	4.3	4.3

Note: Based on all sample population, both ill and non-ill. M = Male, F = Female, T = Total.

Source: Author's calculations from Primary Survey.

Graph 4
Days Ill in Last 6 Months of Small Children (< 6 Years all Population)

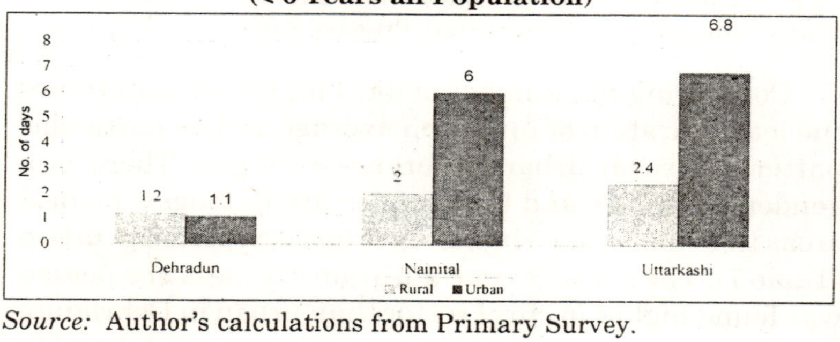

Source: Author's calculations from Primary Survey.

Nearly all the people ill during last six months in sample have received treatment. Majority also took treatment from a qualified allopathic doctor (Table 8). Although forms of treatment did include allopathic unqualified and some small shares of homeopathy or Ayurvedic and home remedies, the preference for allopathic treatment is clear constituting more than 90% cases except urban Uttarkashi. Surprisingly, the distance travelled for treatment is more only for rural Dehradun. In all the districts the time cost is more in rural sector. Although the communication problem in rural regions is reflected, urban people may be travelling more to seek the more suitable treatment due to their awareness about health facilities, transport facilities and economic capability. Absence from active life is more in urban probably for the same reason. The case of Uttarkashi is a reflection of the state of health care. Rural people's relative ignorance of the facilities available and the quality of services availed, for example the real qualification of providers may also be underlying the results.

Table 8
Treatment for Illness

	Dehradun		*Nainital*		*Uttarkashi*	
Name of Disease	*Rural*	*Urban*	*Rural*	*Urban*	*Rural*	*Urban*
Absence (days)	11.1	10.0	11.1	14.5	7.6	12.0
Treated (%)	98.9	100	98.7	98.3	99.7	100
Type of treatment (%)						
Allopathic unqualified	13.6	1.5	23.9	15.5	4.1	27.9
Allopathic Qualified	83.4	94.0	71.3	78.5	93.7	68.9
Homeopathic/ Ayurvedic	0.9	0.5	0.3	0.6	0.5	1.1
Home remedy	0.9	1.5	1.3	1.7	1.1	2.1
Others	0.1	2.5	1.9	2.0	0.3	0.0
Travel						
Distance (Km)	11.6	4.1	10.2	10.8	21.5	24.1
Time (hours)	1.1	0.8	1.3	0.8	2.0	1.4

Note: Based on those reported ill in last 6 months.

Source: Author's calculations from Primary Survey.

Going by a different recall, a little more than 20% of the people reported some illness in the last three months (Table 9). Expense on doctor is by far the lowest component in treatment expense generally less than 1%. Expenditure on medicine is by far the highest among all items followed by travel cost to seek treatment. Rural people have spent more on medicines in all the districts but curiously, urban people spend more on travelling. This speaks of the urban people's choices of medical facilities and the mode of transporting the sick However, travel constitutes a significant part of the medical expenditure in both sectors.

Table 9
Expenditure on Illness in Last 3 months

	Dehradun		*Nainital*		*Uttarkashi*	
	Rural	*Urban*	*Rural*	*Urban*	*Rural*	*Urban*
If ill (%)	24.0	26.7	20.9	22.8	21.0	21.8
Expenditure (Rs)						
Doctor	8	73	5	28	5	8
Medicine	1830	840	1848	1687	3301	1210
Travel	226	264	308	546	277	1251
Total	2064	1177	2161	2261	3583	2469

Note: Based on those reported in last 3 months.
Source: Author's calculations from Primary Survey.

Total expenditure on illness reveals that Rs. 2000 to Rs. 4000 is spent during the period on any illness (Graph 5a). As we have seen this is a sum total of different expenses and does not match the patterns in travel expenses (Graph 5b). In Dehradun and Uttarkashi, rural spending is more than urban but in Nainital expenditure is almost even The health position only finds consolation from the low incidence of illness. The clean environment possibly rescues the people from an unhealthy life in the hilly and difficult terrain. The environment consciousness of the urban people and their demand for sanitation is another positive factor. However there are diseases and

Graph 5a
Expenditure on illness

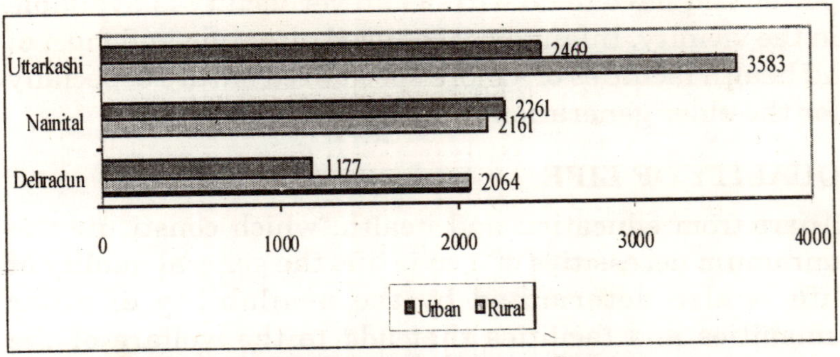

Source: Author's calculations from Primary Survey.

Graph 5b
Travel Cost for Treatment of Ill

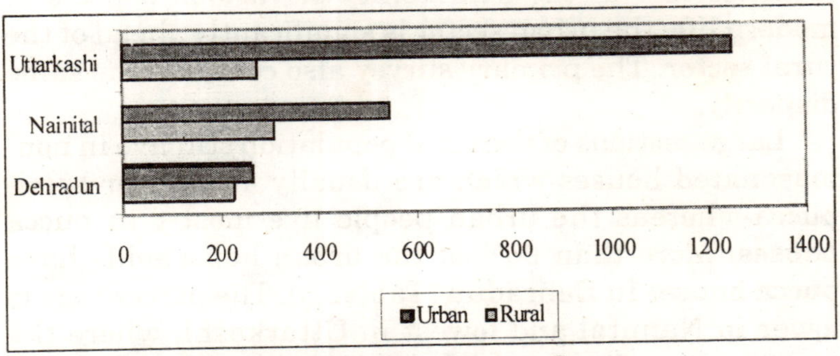

Source: Author's calculations from Primary Survey.

calamities. Both rural and urban people are found to be afflicted by the inadequate health system and the need to travel to more distant facilities of a minimum quality but rural people are greater sufferers due to their difficulty in transport and their poverty. The urban community however had been more vocal of the failure of health system in the time taken, quality of service and cost. It is possible that urban people make longer journeys and pick better health facilities if they have to travel to other states for diagnosis and treatment. The rural people are handicapped by poor communication, lack of information and low spending power and have to do with whatever facility is available in the vicinity. Infant diseases need attention and most of all health facilities of a more specialized nature especially for the elder generation is a lacuna.

QUALITY OF LIFE

Apart from education and health, which constitute the minimum necessities of a civic life, the general quality of life is also determined by the availability of other amenities and facilities that add to the welfare of the household. Secondary data indicated a marked discrepancy in this respect going against the rural sector. In terms of housing and sanitation, communication facilities and in the availability of various aspects of modern life, the urban sector is significantly ahead of the rural sector. The primary survey also confirms the same disparity.

Large sections of the rural population still live in non-masonated houses-which are usually *kuchha* or semi-pucca-whereas the urban people live mostly in pucca houses. More than 90% of the urban households have pucca houses in Dehradun (Table 10). The percentage is lower in Nainital and lowest in Uttarkashi, where the rural urban disparity is much less wide. The non-masonated houses provide little protection from natural hazards and the weather. Living space, which also contributes to the quality of life, is however found to be more ample in the rural sector. There are more households in the rural sector with houses that have multiple rooms, compared to the urban sector. The rural households also have their own homestead land more often than the urban households. Electricity is found to be the main source of energy for lighting in the households, although kerosene and gas are also used occasionally. In fact, a majority of the houses in the state are electrified, but about 20% houses still lack this facility in Nainital and Uttarkashi. Hygienic living requires sewerage and toilet facilities. The state has a very poor record in this context, with 40% to 50% households in rural areas lacking in-house toilets. A small section of the households avail government and community facilities but not less than 37% do not have access to even these facilities. The figure for households without toilets is about 20% in urban areas in Uttarkashi and Dehradun, while the lowest figures (about 8%) are for urban Nainital. The rural urban disparity is also very high in this context, with rural Uttarkashi having the highest share of households that do no have this facility. Drinking water is dominant problem and a large section of the sample households do not have any access to piped water. Rural Dehradun and Nainital are most deficient in this area while the urban sector is more privileged. As a result of the lack of water facilities, use of common water bodies still prevail in rural areas. Use of LPG is limited in rural areas (Dehradun being the largest user) and it is mostly used along with other fuel. Wood is the most important fuel for these people, while kerosene is also used by them. People have to travel from 2 to 4.5 Km in order to get fuel. This problem is most acute in Uttarkashi, where 65% of the households have to travel more than 3 Km in order to get their fuel supplies. The traveling involved in less in the urban areas of the state, although Uttarkashi once again suffers more relative to the other areas.

We also study the difference in the households in terms of their possession of various assets. Some of these assets translate to improved communication and most symbolize technological development. Invariably the rural households report possession less often than their urban counterparts, except for possession of bicycles and radios.

With respect of telephones and mobile phones, the share of urban areas is about double that of in rural areas in Nainital and Uttarkashi. We have also constructed an index of asset holding using Principal Component Analysis. Select assets are considered. In general Dehradun has the highest average asset holding index and Uttarkashi the least. The rural urban disparity in asset holding is clear from this exercise.

Table 10
Quality of Life: Housing, Lighting and Sanitation

	Dehradun		*Nainital*		*Uttarkashi*	
	Rural	*Urban*	*Rural*	*Urban*	*Rural*	*Urban*
Type of House						
Kuchha	18.7	1.7	20.5	5.0	8.6	7.4
Pucca	71.0	92.6	65.3	78.3	63.7	68.0
Without Electricity-Lighting	7.9	3.3	25.5	2.5	17.6	6.6
Without own Toilet *Facility (%)*	39	23.1	41.8	8.3	50.6	20.5
Without Piped tap-Drinking Water	53.1	37.2	60.7	19.2	18.0	11.5
Without LPG fuel	37.0	15.0	57.7	25.8	50.2	20.5
Assets						
Fan	84.2	96.7	59.0	92.5	38.0	80.3
Television	68.5	90.1	54.8	78.3	51.0	83.6
Telephone	24.1	34.7	16.3	30.0	22.9	45.1
Bicycle	61.0	54.5	57.7	40.8	4.9	16.4
Scooter/Motor Cycle	22.8	26.4	17.2	30.8	8.6	23.8

Source: Author's calculations from Primary Survey.

Graph 6
Household Asset Index

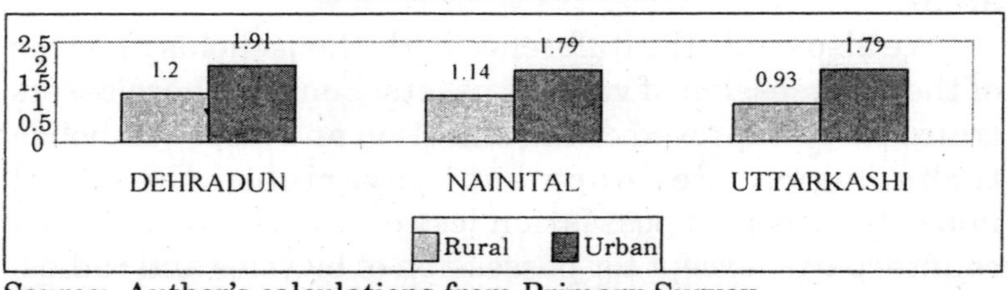

Source: Author's calculations from Primary Survey.

Graph 7
Households without Own Toilet

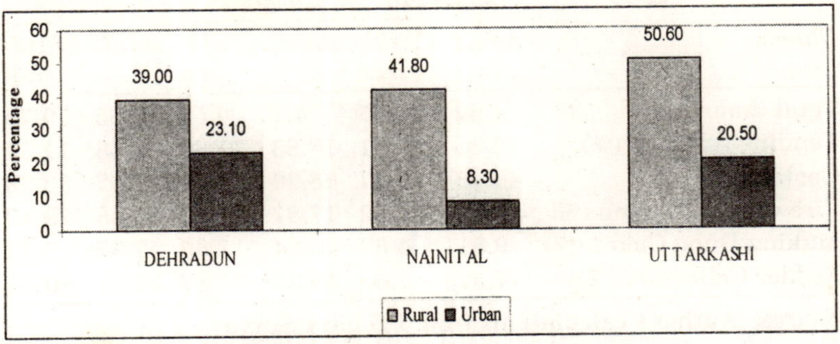

Source: Author's calculations from Primary Survey.

Graph 8
Types of Houses in Three Districts

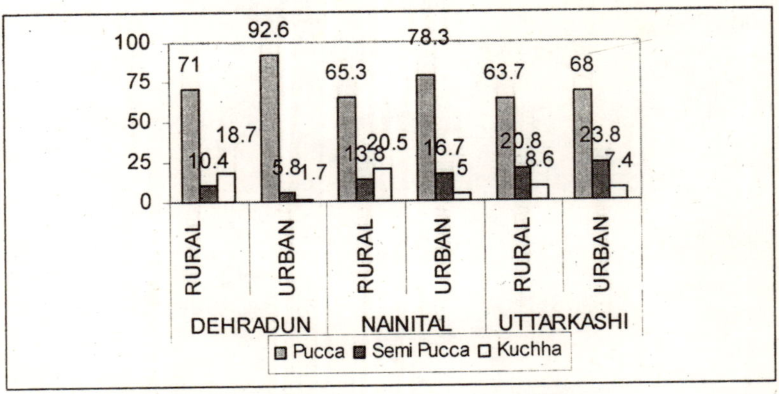

Source: Author's calculations from Primary Survey.

The quality of life of women is significantly determined by the extent of their household drudgery. In Uttarakhand, women spend about 4 hours per day on average on cooking, tending animal, collecting firewood, making dung cakes and collecting fodder. It is higher in Uttarkashi (Table 11).

Table 11
Time Spent by Women

Chores	*Dehradun*		*Nainital*		*Uttarkashi*	
	Adult	*Children*	*Adult*	*Children*	*Adult*	*Children*
Total (hours/day)	4.62	0.65	4.7	0.59	6.65	0.78
Tending Animals (%)	12.34	12.31	13.83	11.86	11.58	11.54
Cooking(%)	40.48	50.77	38.30	37.29	27.67	33.33
Firewood Collection (%)	20.56	24.62	17.87	27.12	30.38	29.49
Making Dung Cakes (%)	9.31	4.62	10.64	11.86	7.97	5.13
Fodder Collection (%)	17.32	7.69	19.36	11.86	22.41	20.51

Source: Author's calculations from Primary Survey.

Other than cooking, firewood collection consumes a large part (about 20%) of their time. This share is larger in Uttarkashi. Girl children also contribute to these chores with the total time spent being slightly less than an hour.

7

RURAL URBAN RELATIONS IN UTTARAKHAND: RETROSPECT AND PROSPECT

The new Himalayan state of Uttarakhand, which was carved out of Uttar Pradesh, is a combination of strengths and weaknesses that are distinct from other states in the plains. The hilly terrain and ecology prevents input intensive and high productivity agriculture from penetrating the region and modern industrialization from being successful. It carries the historical weakness of having been part of the largest state in India, which had its own set of problems. The state is predominantly rural, and hence suffers from the handicaps that traditionally afflict a rural society. On the other hand, Uttarakhand has a cleaner and more pristine environment compared to other states and prides itself for being situated in the majestic Himalayan mountains. This allows the state to attract tourists to its national parks, forests and religious sites and offers possibilities of exclusive activities. The state also has significant potential for horticulture and hydroelectric power generation.

This chapter attempts to bring together the findings of the study, from both secondary information and primary field survey. A summary of the findings is followed by aggregate analyses to (i) quantify rural urban disparity and compare primary with secondary based evidences (ii) look for the sectoral linkages and the urban influence on rural development.

In the following sections, we have compiled the findings from our primary survey, from the secondary data and from our discussions with concerned people and provided a commentary on rural urban development in the state.

DEVELOPMENT SCENARIO IN UTTARAKHAND

Income and Consumption

The districts are highly uneven in their contribution to total output in the state. The more urbanized districts of Nainital, Dehradun, Haridwar and US Nagar have relatively high District Domestic Product (DDP) and a very large share of output while the predominantly rural districts have low levels of output. The Net State Domestic Product (NSDP) comes mostly from the primary sector and agriculture while industry has the smallest contribution. The developed districts contribute to both agriculture and industry because of their marketing and infrastructure. This skewness is thus a prominent feature in the spatial and industry wise picture of production in the state.

The NSS data on consumption expenditure available separately for rural and urban areas shows that there is income and consumption disparity between these two sectors as elsewhere in the country, but the disparity is narrowing at all levels. The rural urban inequality measured in terms of the Monthly Per Capita Expenditure (MPCE) shows a declining tendency. The poor are concentrated in non-agriculture work force and benefit more by the overall growth process than rural specific development programmes. The performance of urban sector has been comparatively less satisfactory. The primary survey finds rural urban disparities in household incomes and poor income potential of occupations like agriculture, agricultural labour and agro-processing.

Demography

The state has improved in terms of the usual vital indicators i.e., Crude Birth Rate (CBR), Crude death Rate (CDR) and Infant Mortality rate (IMR) and is above the all-India level. The rural sector however has a weaker record in terms of all these demographic indicators and needs the attention of policy-makers. The sex ratio in the state is favourable to females and more so in the rural and hilly districts and in the rural sectors. But this is also an outcome of out-migration and the adverse sex ratio in the 0-6 years age group raises question about the actual status of women in this state.

Employment

As expected, agriculture is the main occupation in rural area while other occupations dominate the urban sector. Although the distribution of occupation is highly skewed, there is some diversification away from agriculture. The primary survey shows that agriculture is not the largest provider of household earnings. Salaried employment is found to be much more lucrative and many services are coming up as alternative sources of employment. The rural youth in the state prefer non-farm employment to agriculture. The unemployment registered in employment exchange throws up a staggering figure of over three lakh. The survey found unemployment to be a serious problem with most young people in agriculture, many of whom have education and training, looking for a job outside agriculture. Female unemployment in rural areas is also serious. The people are extremely interested in self-employment but they want training and marketing facilities for pursuing this end.

The work participation ratio has fallen in Uttarakhand in comparison to the all-India level and there is an increase in the marginalisation of the worker. Work participation is higher in the rural districts and in the rural sectors of the districts. Women participate more as cultivators and agricultural labour in rural sector and often as unpaid family workers.

Education

Primary education has been a neglected area for a long time. However, in the last decade or so, emphasis has been given on school education, particularly at the elementary stage. This effort can be judged in terms of school facilities, access, actual enrolment etc., but the outcome in terms of attracting and retaining the school-aged children is also important. Census data reveal remarkable literacy levels in Uttarakhand, surpassing the all-India level. There is however a rural urban disparity with a gender gap, highlighting the need for increased schooling in villages with emphasis on the female child. The NCERT survey shows distribution of schools in favour of primary level and with no clear discrimination against the rural sector. The literacy rate is high, above 80% for rural males but falls for females in both sectors. In the urban district of Haridwar and US Nagar, both genders share a low literacy.

The primary survey shows promising results despite lingering of rural urban disparity. There has been remarkable spread in education among recent generation (19-25 years) and particularly among the rural women. Moreover in the elementary age 5-14 there is nearly complete enrolment and minimum dropouts but a small section of children have stayed out of the systems. Apart from formal schooling, communication media including TV and newspaper are important in educating the people. One crucial test of the success of education is the employment opportunity that education can fetch. Exposure to IT in education needs improvement. There is a complaint about difficulty of availing higher education and sometime people prefer private schools at the primary level on grounds of quality and the language that is used as a medium of teaching.

Health

Secondary data availability on health facilities is inadequate in Uttarakhand. Reproductive and Child Health (RCH) data indicates insufficiency of both curative and preventive facilities. Ante-natal care, deliveries, child and infant mortality, immunization and women's health care all are worse in the rural sector compared to the urban sector. There is a shortage of health centers and hospitals, of good doctors and facilities, in the whole state let alone individual villages. Above all, purchase of medicines has become costly to village people. The information on existing facilities does not say much about its quality, although there are complaints about them from the surveyed villages. The rural areas have a clean environment. However, sanitation is lacking in these areas. There is no great rural urban disparity in the incidence of various diseases or the duration of illness. The cost of illness in terms of duration and expenditure is higher in Uttarkashi, perhaps due to the mountainous terrain. In the rural areas, the elderly population suffers more than the young ones. Urban areas seem to be experiencing the same unsatisfactory health situation. However, rural people have very little ability to seek health-care if it is available outside the state and end up spending more, in contrast to urban people who are more privileged in information and resources and capable of traveling greater distances to get the appropriate facility. The poor transport situation makes the disparity all the more worse. The government needs to improve the health centers, supply adequate doctors and provide more specialist facility especially for the aged who suffers more illness. The burden of buying prescribed medicine is a problem that deserves consideration. Private facilities often replace the missing public presence and rural people avail of private services at higher cost. There may be scope for public private partnership to make the service affordable. Satellite based technology holds a promise in taking medical services and information to remote areas.

Quality of Life

The difference in the quality of life between rural and urban areas is well known. The two sectors differ in housing, water, electricity supply and amenities with a clear bias against the rural sector. Both secondary and primary data confirm this disparity for the state of Uttarakhand. Sanitation is still a neglected area in villages. Rural people live more often with primitive housing, no bathroom or toilets and untreated drinking water. The women travel to fetch fodder and wood, the latter being a dominant fuel as the use of LPG is still not widely practiced in the villages. People hardly have modern amenities like television and telephone. The urban people too complain about sanitation and drinking water that are managed inefficiently by local bodies. However, they manage to get better service by being vocal about the poor performance of the elected bodies and their responsibilities. Similar actions undertaken by the Panchayati Raj Institutions (PRI) will help villages.

Infrastructure and Resources

Uttarakhand is well endowed in natural resources consisting of scenic beauty, minerals, forests, wild life and water. There is substantial potential for power generation due to the water resources. However, the ecology of the state renders most development projects subject to extreme caution for their sustainability impacts. Connectivity is mostly through roads while hydel power is the main energy source and both of these receive priority from the government. As of now though, roads are inadequate, village electrification is incomplete and not all households can use electricity, especially due to their remoteness. Villages have poor telephone access, which is a severe communication handicap. As far as banks are concerned around 50% of the served villages have access to them.

Agriculture and Rural Development

Uttarakhand is an agricultural state. However only 12% area in the hilly state is available for cultivation and 65% is forested. The cultivating households expressed the need for improvement in the irrigation facilities. Fertilizer use is low due to the nature of the terrain and poor distribution outlets, but this deficiency raises the prospect of organic farming with export prospects. However, productivity is low and training and extension is required in this regard. Cash crops like soya bean cultivation hold promise. Agricultural development in a trained and eco-friendly framework should be combined with processing, packing and information system to promote rural development and self-employment among women.

RURAL URBAN DISPARITY, LINKAGES AND IMPACT OF DISTANCE

The disparities noted from the study are quantitatively summarized in Table 1 that also presents the results from the primary and secondary data sources together. The primary data based results are drawn from the sample collected in this project and refers to three particular districts in the state whereas the secondary data drawn from Census 2001 describe the state as a whole. Similarly the Table also presents results from other state level surveys conducted by government organizations namely the NFHS and the NSSO.

The sectoral disparity in education, measured by the urban-rural ratio (urban performance for every 1% performance in rural sector) in literacy rate, is found to be against the rural sector from both sources. However, it is less at 1.06 from primary results (based on Dehradun, Nainital and Uttarkashi) compared to 1.17 shown by Census data on Uttarakhand. In the primary survey, Nainital stands out in rural literacy although that for the urban population is low among all the three districts. Considering gender, once again rural Nainital and urban Uttarkashi lead over the other regions. Rural female literacy from primary survey at 68% appears much better than 56% reported by Census and 55% by NFHS for the state. However the figures for the urban sector are comparable between the different data sources. Considering women who crossed primary education threshold, the survey shows better performance of rural areas and a lower disparity compared to NFHS data. The share of women with schooling completed is low in the rural sector (above 10% only in Dehradun). The survey shows that it is also poor in the urban sector and this is consistent with the findings from the NFHS data.

A village or a town can be said to have access to any infrastructure facility if there is availability of the facility in the proximity. Here, access is defined in terms of having the facility within five km in the case of post office and public telephone and within the village for other facilities. The urban centers surveyed all have access to roads (pucca including highways), transport facilities like bus station, railway station or airport, post office and public telephone. Access varies in villages with respect of transport with 22% of villages having roads and 6% having transport facilities. Both villages and urban centers seem to have access post office and public telephone. Health facility

Table 1

Rural Urban Disparities from Primary and Secondary Information: Summary Statistics

Development Indicators	*Primary Survey in Three Districts*								*Uttarakhand*				*Secondary data source*
	Uttarkashi		*Nainital*		*Dehradun*		*Total*		*Secondary*		*NFHS Survey 1998-99*		
	Rural	*Urban*	*Rural*	*Urban*	*Rural*	*Urban*	*Rural*	*Urban*	*Rural*	*Urban*	*Rural*	*Urban*	
Literate (•)	78	89	80	77	78	87	79	84	70	82	-	-	Census 2001
Female Literate (•)	64	81	72	72	69	79	68	77	56	75	55	81	Census 2001
Primary and Above	43	58	46	48	47	55	45	54	-	-	36	68	
							45	54			39	68	
School complete	7	18	6	16	11	13	8	16	-	-	5	32	
Access to Infrastructure (1)													
Roads (2)	33	100	17	100	33	100	22	100	-	-	-	-	
Transport Facility (3)	17	100	0	100	0	100	6	100	-	-	-	-	
Post office (4)	100	100	100	100	100	100	100	100	39	10	-	-	UA at a Glance 2005
Public Telephone	100	100	100	100	100	100	100	100	-	-	33	10	-
All Health Institutions (4)	33	100	0	100	67	100	33	100			36	4	
Housing (5)													

Contd...

Development Indicators	Primary Survey in Three Districts								Uttarakhand				Secondary data source
	Uttarkashi		Nainital		Dehradun		Total		Secondary		NFHS Survey 1998-99		
	Rural	Urban	Rural	Urban	Rural	Urban	Rural	Urban	Rural	Urban	Rural	Urban	
Good andLiveable (6)	84	92	79	95	81	98	82	95	96	97	78	91	Census 2001
Electricity	82	93	75	98	92	97	83	96	50	91	39	92	Census 2001
Toilet (7)	49	80	58	92	61	77	56	83	32	87	22	87	Census 2001
Drinking water (8)	84	96	88	90	95	93	89	93	80	95	-	-	Census 2001
	44	55	77	51	38	41	53				Near premises		
											Near premises		
Income (9)	631	1273	707	1378	905	1332	748	1327	551	836	-	-	NSSO 1999-00.

Notes: (•) Literate includes only schooled population in Primary data (above 5 years).

(1) Access is there when facility exists within 5 km distance for Post office and Public telephone and within village for others. Primary data give % rural/urban centers.

(2) Primary data give rural pucca road and highway.

(3) Bus station, Railways station and Airport.

(4) Primary and Secondary data give respectively the access and the number per lakh of population.

(5) Percentage of houses

(6) Primary and NFHS data give Pucca and semi-pucca houses.

(7) Own toilet.

(8) Primary data give own and public source and secondary give near or within premises.

(9) Rs Per capita per month, Primary data are for income (converted) and secondary are consumption expenditure.

Source: Survey, Census, NSS, NFHS, RCH.

constitutes an important social infrastructure but comparison is difficult with differing standards set for rural and urban sectors. Adding up all health care institutions based on NFHS data, there seems to be only 4 institutions per lakh of population in the towns compared to 36 in the villages. The primary data also show proximity of some health center in all cases except for villages of Uttarkashi. However, one third of the villages seem to have no facility within the village. Overall however, the statistics do not imply an advantage favouring the rural sector since the standard, size and quality of the urban institution is not comparable to the rural ones. According to the view of the people from the rural interviews, the public centers–even if they exist-usually are inadequate in terms of staff and facilities and rural people have to depend on urban facilities even for minor illnesses. Shortage of specialized facilities in the urban centers deprives the rural people as much as the urban people.

The quality of life is characterized by the quality of the houses, electrification, drinking water and toilet facility. Since data sources provide differing categorization, the share of population with semi-pucca and pucca housing is compared with those without such facilities, from the survey and the Census and NFHS data. The primary survey indicates that 81 to 84% of rural houses and 92 to 98% of urban houses in the three districts are pucca or semi-pucca with a rural average of 82% and urban average of 95%. The rural figure is higher than the NFHS figure of 78% and less than Census figure of 96%, the urban rural ratio being 1.16. Toilet facility is present in less than 50% of rural houses in Uttarkashi while the percentage is highest in Dehradun. In the urban sector, the share is 80 to 92% in the three cases. The result however is better than the other two sources with a lower urban rural ratio. Drinking water (private or public) within close proximity is present for over 84% rural houses with a maximum of 95% in Dehradun. For the urban sector, the share exceeds 90% in each case. The rural average is 89%, better than Census result of 80%. About 83% of rural houses have electricity connection in the sample, again better than secondary result at the state level but urban result at above 90% is comparable. The villages of Dehradun district appear to have some advantage in civic facilities.

In terms of income (rupees per capita per month), Dehradun records the highest rural income but in the urban sector it comes second by a small margin to Nainital. Comparing these values at the state level with the consumption expenditure computed from the NSSO data of 1999-00, we find that the latter is less in each case. The urban-rural income ratio based on NSSO data is 1.5, and this is less than the income ratio given by the primary survey at 1.8.

The rural urban disparity studied by comparing the two distinct sectors is not adequate in capturing the disparity since rural areas are influenced by the urban centers and the level of influence varies from area to area. The influence level may generate differences in development level across villages. One indicator of the urban influence could be taken as the distance from the urban centers. In order to study this effect, we construct correlation coefficients between the distance and various development indicators, for the sample villages, both at the district level and for the combined data. To the extent that urban sector is expected to influence the development of a village, the correlation is expected to be negative implying that the village near the town will be more developed than the more remote one. However this need not be so due to two reasons. First rural development programmes of the government also play a part and remote villages may be (and usually are) priority and thereby showing better achievement depending on the effectiveness of public action. Second, Uttarakhand is a hilly and largely a rural state and the economy is heavily primary based with the usual large industries playing a small role. Moreover, tourism is a dominant occupation and spread throughout the state. There are some grounds to hope that the rural sector and distant villages may out-perform the other one in some respects.

The computed correlation coefficients (Table 2) do not always have the same signs but in most cases the positive effect of proximity is indicated. The exceptions include the income indicators (0.03 for all sources and 0.36 for agriculture), toilet facility (0.02) and public drinking water (0.39). The latter two may reflect some success in public action in civic provisions though the value is small for toilet provision. Average household income has a small but positive correlation but agricultural income has a larger positive one. Although literacy has the expected negative correlation (-0.25) higher education shows a small but positive correlation (of 0.09) suggesting that people thirsting for education do overcome the barrier of distance.

The rural and urban sectors are components making up the integral whole of the state. The people of the rural sector depend on urban centers for various purposes and cannot generally operate as self–sufficient communities. The rural urban linkages are found to be based on various types of interactions. Perhaps the most important linkage is in terms of employment. Most households in the villages depend on some non-agricultural source of income, as agriculture is not a profitable source of income particularly in the hilly areas. The villagers are reported to travel out of village for their vocation in most cases. About 50% to 60% of the service providers, 20% of the salaried and government service holders and 70% of industrial employees are reported to commute from villages. The mobility in terms of economic activity is observed for all

Table 2
Correlation Between Distance from Urban Center and Development Indicator

District	*Literate %*	*School Complete %*	*AAHI Resident Rs*	*AAHI Agriculture Rs*	*Houses Livable %*	*Houses with Toilet %*	*Houses with Drinking water Private %*	*Houses with Drinking water Public %*	*Houses with Electricity %*
Uttarkashi	-0.45	0.08	-0.56	0.18	-0.68	-0.46	-0.84	0.54	-0.03
Nainital	-0.87	-0.08	0.42	0.75	0.38	0.40	0.90	-0.48	0.00
Dehradun	-0.04	-0.02	-0.58	-0.31	-0.32	-0.21	-0.75	0.76	-0.42
Total	-0.25	0.09	0.03	0.36	-0.21	0.02	-0.36	0.39	-0.01

Note: AAHI is Annual average household income

Source: Author's calculations from Primary Survey.

districts but is higher for Uttarkashi with respect to services and industrial employment

Table 3
Rural Households (%)
Deriving some Income from Outside the Village

	Traditional services	*Modern services*	*Salaried services*	*Governments ervices*	*Large industry*
Uttarkashi	81.8	33.3	3.1	18	83.3
Nainital	33.3	75	20.9	26.1	66.7
Dehradun	12.5	75	29.9	39.4	50
Total	50	63.6	19.2	26.4	69.2

Source: Author's calculations from Primary Survey.

Another important linkage is in the context of education, with the rural people having to send their children to cities and towns for higher level of schooling and education. This is due to the fact that although primary schooling is developed in villages and most villages have access to them, only few villages have a middle school, very few have high school and none have colleges. The demand for health services is a third link with superior health facilities being available only urban areas and villages often not having the minimum necessary medical facilities in terms of staff, medicine or equipment. Many rural people have to travel to the towns even for minor illnesses. Some villages have more costly private facilities. Primary facility exists in 30 % villages but even they are of low standards. Fourthly, both for purchases and sales, the rural people depend on urban markets. These include both business visits and household visits for domestic purchases. Although all the villages are found to be uniformly endowed with their local *kirana* shop and PDS outlets, but lack in markets and mandis make them dependent on urban areas. Fifthly, in order to travel long distances, the rural people have to first go to the urban centers in order to get access to bus or railway stations.

The sample in the three districts surveyed has shown slightly better performance in the whole state compared to secondary sources in many respects. But within the sample, performances and weaknesses are found to vary among the districts and even within a district among the villages surveyed. Comparing the performances with the average or considering the endowment of the villages in different facilities some villages in the three districts can be identified for their areas of weakness.

Rural Urban Relation

Uttarakhand does not boast of metropolitan or very large cities. Rural urban disparities in the state can only be studied in the context of the character of the urban centers and the relationship between rural and urban areas existing in the state. In order to compare the rural and urban development in the state, the following points have to be kept in mind, i.e., (i) many areas that have become urban due to recent conversion retain their rural character (ii) urban population is sometimes only a spillover of the rural population that have migrated to these areas, often leaving their families behind (iii) rural households derive income from members having employment in the urban areas and (iv) there is a strongly geographic dimension to the rural urban distinction in the state. Hence, rather than viewing the rural sector in isolation, the age-old rural urban linkages must be utilized to make Uttarakhand a developed state, and the two sectors must move hand in hand as partners in this development.

Uttarakhand has 74% of its population in rural areas and in many districts, more than 90% of population is rural. With population growth, the number of towns has increased, giving fillip to the urbanization of the state. Geography is a big factor in determining the urbanization of Uttarakhand. The plain districts have turned out to be more urban, more populated and more developed while most hill districts remained rural, agriculture based and less economically developed. The populated districts in the plains encouraged the creation of public facilities and infrastructure. At the other extreme, the inaccessible, sparse and scattered population in the rural areas in the hills has slowed down the process of market formation and discouraged government developmental programs in these areas. Many other aspects of development are influenced by these factors and the severity of this obstacle can be overcome only by determined government effort. The role of public action in the balanced development of this state is therefore more important than in the plains where the market is more effective as a means for achieving development.

Of course, the disparities between the more urbanised districts (that are partly in the plains) and the hilly rural districts are sharp, but disparities within the districts and within the surveyed clusters are also evident. Household incomes, employment opportunities, literacy, health facilities and civic amenities are areas in which the villages fall behind as usual. However, the secondary data that incorporates an intertemporal comparison over a decade, finds no conclusive evidence of a growth in the disparity. In fact, there has been commendable diffusion of school education and new avenues of earning have contributed to rural incomes. However, this convergence comes with little dynamism emerging in the urban regions. Clearly, this is an untenable situation and concerted policy effort needs to be made to make both rural and urban areas an integral part of the growth process.

Development planning in Uttarakhand can be made effective only by keeping in mind the specificities of the state. The state has rightly identified the following areas of emphasis in its course of planning, i.e., (i) roads and communication (ii) eco-friendly economic activities which are forest based, organic, food processing (iii) education and (iv) rural development programme. The state and its budget should give particular attention to (i) health and (ii) employment. The other areas of concern are (i) urban development (ii) gender issue and sex ratio (iii) quality of services, education, health and power and (iv) higher education and training. While narrowing rural-urban disparity is welcome, more attention to the overall development of the state is necessary since the development in the two sectors is linked. The state needs to look into unemployment problem, promote self-employment, service skills and women's enterprise through necessary finance, infrastructure and training. The sex ratio in rural sector is positive but this is an outcome of out-migration. The adverse sex ratio in the 0-6 years age group raises question about the actual status of females in this state. Government may look into the possibility of promoting village level higher education, distance education through remote sensing and making transport easier and safer for students to commute. The government needs to improve the health centers, supply adequate doctors and provide more specialist facility, especially for the aged who suffers more from illnesses. Partnership with private sector and use of technology could be carefully designed to provide this crucial facility. More active role of the PRI's and people's participation will help villages, especially in procuring civic amenities. Lastly, agricultural development may be combined with processing, packaging and information technology to promote robust rural development.

REFERENCES

Akita, T., R.A. Lukman and Y. Yamada (1999), 'Inequality in the Distribution of Household Expenditures in Indonesia: A Theil Decomposition Analysis', *The Developing Economies,* XXXVII-2, 197-221.

Balisacan, A.M. and N. Fuwa (2003), 'Is Spatial Income Inequalty Increasing in The Philippines?' Paper prepared for the UNU/WIDER project *conference on Spatial Inequality in Asia.*

Bhattacharya, B.B. and S. Sakthivel (2003) 'Regional Disparities in Growth: A Comparison of Pre and Post-Reform Period', *Discussion Paper No. 73/2003,* Institute of Economic Growth, Delhi.

Census of India (1981), Town and Village Directory.

Census of India (1991), Population Total.

Census of India (2001), Uttaranchal Provisional Population Totals, Series-6, Paper 1.

Census of India (2001), Uttaranchal Provisional Population Totals, Series-6, Paper 3.

Census of India (*www.censusindia.net*)

Centre for Monitoring Indian Economy Pvt. Ltd., October 2000, *Profiles of Districts.*

Chakravarty Sukhamoy (1987), *Development Planning: The Indian Experience,* Clarendon Press, Oxford.

Dasgupta, Partha (2001) *Human Well-Being and the Natural Environment* Oxford, New York.

Datt, Gaurav (1998), Poverty in India and Indian States: An Update *The Indian Journal of Labour Economics,* Vol. 41 No. 2.

Deaton, Angus (2001), Adjusted Indian Poverty Estimates for 1999-2000, *Sarvekshana,* Vol. xx14 Oct., 2000-Mar 2001.

Deaton, A. and J. Dreze, (2002), 'Poverty and Inequality in India' *Economic and Political Weekly* September.

Dreze, Jean and Amartya Sen (2004), *India Development and Participation,* Oxford.

Furman, J. and J.E. Stiglitz (1998), 'Economic Consequences of Income Inequality', *Federal Reserve Bank of Kansus City,* Journal Proceedings.

Government of India, Family Welfare Statistics in India-2006.

Government of Uttaranchal, Department of Health and Family Welfare and the Futures Group International, New Delhi, (2002) *Reproductive Child Health and Population Policy issues in Uttaranchal Workshops Proceeding.*

Gulati, A. and T. Kelley (1999), *Trade Liberalisation and Indian Agriculture,* Oxford University Press, New Delhi.

International Institute for Population Sciences, 1998-99, *National Family Health Survey India*

Jagarn Research Center (JRC, 2005), Uttaranchal and Uttar Pradesh at Glance.

Johnson, Craig, Priya Deshingkar and Daniel Start (2005), "Grounding the State: Devolution and Development in India's Panchayats" *The Journal of Development Studies*, Vol. 41, No. 6, August.

Joshi, P.C. (1995), *Uttarakhand: Issues and Challenges,* Har-Anand Publications, New Delhi.

Juyal, Pooja (2002), "Status of Women and Gender Issues in Uttaranchal" in *Reproductive Child Health and Population Policy issues in Uttaranchal.*

Kar, Sabyasachi and S. Sakthivel (2003), "Regional divergence in India during the era of Liberalization: A Sectoral Decomposition" , *Working Paper* of the Institute of Economic Growth.

Kar, Sabyasachi (2007), "Inclusive Growth in Hilly Regions: Priorities for the Uttarakhand Economy" *Working Paper* of the Institute of Economic Growth.

Krugman, P. and R. Livas Elizondo (1996), 'Trade Policy and the Third World Metropolis', *Journal of Development Economics*, 49,1, pp. 137-50,

Kuznets, S. (1955), Economic Growth and Income Inequality, *The American Economic Review*, XLV (1).

Lewis, W.A. (1954), Economic Development with Unlimited Supplies of Labour, Manchester School.

Lipton, M. (1977), *'Why Poor People Stay Poor: Urban Bias in World Development'*, Cambridge, Harvard University Press.

Minhas, Jain and Tendulkar (1991), Declining incidence of Poverty in the 1980s, *EPW*, July 6-13.

Mitra, A. and P. S. Bhattacharya (2000), 'Industry-Urban Nexus, Employment and Poverty: A Quantitative Assessment," Paper Presented at the *Conference in honour of K.L. Krishna, Delhi School of Economics*, December.

Myrdal, Gunnar (1957), *Economic Theory and Under-developed Regions,* Gerald Duckworth & Co. Ltd.

Nurkse, Ragnar (1953), *Problems of Capital Formation in under Developed Countries,* Oxford.

Population Foundation of India, New Delhi.

National Sample Survey Organisation (various) *Sarvekshana.*

Ravillion Martin (2002), Poverty Comparisons *The World Bank.*

Sahn and Stifel (2002), 'Urban-Rural Inequality in Africa' Paper prepared for the UNU/WIDER project conference on Spatial Inequality in Africa.

Sen, Abhijit and Himanshu (2004), Poverty and Inequality in India *Economic and Political Weekly,* September 18.

Sen, Amartya (1974), *Poverty, Inequality and Unemployment: some Conceptual Issues in measurement in T.N. Srinivasan and P.K. Bardhan* (ed) *Poverty and Income distribution in India*, Statistical Publishing Society.

Sen, Amartya (2003), India *Development and Participation* Oxford.

Sen, Amartya (1999), *Development as Freedom*, Oxford.

Shorrocks, Anotony and Guangua Wan (2004), Spatial Decomposition of Inequality, Wider

Sharma, Suresh, Nilabja Ghosh (2007), "Education for All in Rural Himalayas: A Case Study of Uttarakhand' Institute of Economic Growth, Working Paper Series no. E/284/2007.

Sharma, Suresh (2007), "Immunization Coverage in India' Institute of Economic Growth, Working Paper Series no E/283/2007.

State Government Data (www.ua.nic.in/aises/vifirfa)

State Planning Department, Govt. of Uttarakhand.

Sundaram, K. and Suresh D. Tendulkar (2003), Poverty has declined in the *'1999' Economic and Political Weekly,* XXXVIII (4).

Tsakloglou, P. (1993), 'Aspects of Inequality in Greece', *Journal of Development Economics*, 40, 53-7.

Vakulabharanam, Vamsi (2005), " Growth and Distress in South Indian Peasant Economy During the Era of Economic Liberalisation" *The Journal of Development Studies*, Vol. 41, No. 6, August.

World Bank (2001), *World Development Report: Attacking Poverty,* New York, Oxford University Press.

World Bank (2004), *World Development Report: Making Services Work for Poor People,* New York, Oxford University Press.

INDEX